The Anxiety Chronicles:

39 Real-life Stories of Personal Angst,
Honesty, Humour & Coping

Dr. Rick Thomas

ambient.inc.

ambient consulting, inc.
Vancouver, British Columbia, Canada

Thomas, Richard B. (Rick), 1961 –
The Anxiety Chronicles: 39 real-life stories of personal angst, honesty, humour & coping /
Rick Thomas.

Also issued in electronic format.
ISBN: **978-0-9867420-0-2**

Publisher:
ambient consulting, inc.
Vancouver, British Columbia, Canada

Web page: http://www.ambientconsulting.ca
E-mail: rick@ambientconsulting.ca

For ordering information visit http://theanxietychronicles.com or
rick@ambientconsulting.ca

Author Photo: David Pasca
Cover and Inside Illustrations: Garry Brooks

The Anxiety Chronicles:

*39 Real-life Stories of Personal Angst,
Honesty, Humour & Coping*

I dedicate this book to my partner
who tirelessly shares in my anxiety;
my Father, the 'worry wart',
and
to everyone who can relate.

Contents

Acknowledgements

With gratitude . . .

I hold deep gratitude for the many people who have assisted me in the realization of this book.

I thank Dr. Howard Koseff for writing the final chapter of the book; it provides us with informed and meaningful information and suggestions for dealing with anxiety.

I would also like to thank Garry Brooks who, through his talent, added so significantly to this book by way of his illustrations.

To my editor, Naava Smolash, a heartfelt *thank you* for your keen eye and guidance.

Although only a fraction of the stories received are reflected in these pages, I would like to express my sincere gratitude to all of the people who responded to my anxiety survey and shared their own stories of angst, honesty, humour and coping with me. You were my inspiration!

Introduction

I have always had anxiety... at least as far back as I can
remember. I inherited it from my father; thanks, Dad! My father
was a worrywart, and that manifested in all sorts of behaviours,
both embarrassing (calling friends' parents if we weren't home at
exactly the right time), and not so embarrassing because we were
unawares until our mother let us in on the secret (pacing...
nervous snacking... and conjuring up scenarios of doom that – in
the end – never came to pass). Of course, my brother, sister and I
had to adapt and deal with Dad's anxious idiosyncrasies in one
creative way or another as we grew up.

Well, that was a long time ago now, and I am embarrassed to say,
but comfortable enough to admit, that I live some of those exact
behaviours. My poor partner. I do so, not with pride but with the
knowledge and awareness that enables me, at least, to reflect

back, smile, and realize that Dad did the best he could. I have to tell you at this point that we were good kids, *really*!

I've experienced a lot of symptoms related to anxiety: cold sweats, rapid heartbeat, elevated blood pressure, knots in the stomach, nausea. I have even experienced what is known as an anxiety attack. I survived. However, I still to this day experience pangs of anxiety.

One of my health care providers – somewhere between a naturopath and a homeopath – even told me that I have an "anxious body": that I hold anxiety within my physical body. You know, I can understand that. Our bodies are amazing systems; mine just happens to be a vessel for anxiety. Funny!

Well…

I'd be surprised to find anyone who has not experienced anxiety of some sort at some moment in their life. This is not a challenge, but a generalization that offers a space for us to be OK with the fact that we all experience worry, trepidation or anxiousness as part of the natural flow of our lives.

The idea to write a book like this has been germinating for several years. I've been thinking about anxiety (my Dad's and my own) and its impact on our bodies (physical and emotional) for about ten years now, and thought that I'd like to gather some other peoples' stories of anxiety and coping that I could share, hoping that these stories would allow all of us who read them to smile and realize that we are not alone in living and dealing with our 'issues'. Perhaps along with sharing a laugh, I and my readers can learn some new or different ways of coping.

I originally titled the book *Urinal Anxiety* – after one of the scenarios described within – until I realized that this working title would not attract the masses (here's hoping). Thus the change to the current title. My aim with the book is to share common stories from common people who experience anxiety every day, and who – at least for some – have put methods into place to allow them to cope. As you will quickly notice, it is not a book about the science of anxiety. There are several volumes already written on the subject.

I am very thankful to Dr. Howard Koseff for his chapter that truly completes the book. His wisdom and knowledge about anxiety and his 'bellybreathe' method to relieve anxiety works, at least for me. I encourage you to take stock of his short chapter; his suggestions are worth your consideration.

Enjoy the read. I know the subject is a serious one, and there are plenty of books that do the topic great justice. This book is meant to create lightness around the topic of anxiety, and, I hope, around the anxiety that you or your loved ones experience. I hope it puts a smile on your face through the realization that each of the scenarios describes hundreds – if not thousands – of people affected by anxiety just like us.

Rick Thomas, EdD

Abbey – *G r o c e r y S t o r e F l y e r A n x i e t y*

Abbey gathered up the Friday newspapers and made her way to the kitchen table. She sat in the chair that looked out onto her garden. She liked Friday nights, she noticed, as she pondered to herself for a moment. The kids were out amusing themselves, playing with other children in the cul-de-sac. Daniel, her husband, was tending to the lawn, keeping the weekend free for family fun.

Abbey had a good two hours to herself. She set aside this time each Friday night as her alone time – time that she could spend examining all of the grocery flyers for the best shopping deals for the upcoming week. And Abbey was a pro at getting the best deals! In fact, she prided herself on it. Whether it was toilet paper or ground chuck, frozen popsicles or washing detergent, she didn't pay full price for anything unless she was forced to, especially for something that she knew regularly went on sale. In fact, she would become quite upset if she missed a special or bonus offer, or if she missed the opportunity to get extra travel or gift points, which often happened.

Abbey thought of herself as a 'modern' woman. However, she still found comfort in having fully stocked shelves and a freezer that contained every cut of meat, fish or poultry known to man: frozen pizzas, pies, fruit – you name it, she had it. It made her feel like she was fulfilling her role as a good wife and mother.

Abbey shopped at two grocery stores on Saturday mornings. In her view of the world, this was the only way she could assure herself that she was in the position to get the best possible deals, period. It was still a nuisance, however, that one of the two stores had moved its sales week from Sunday to Sunday to Saturday to Saturday, which, as a result, didn't match the sales day of her other grocery store. "What a pain!" she blurted out loud, looking over her shoulder, forgetting that she was alone. Because of this change, and because of the fact that she always did her grocery shopping early Saturday mornings (she was not a day-to-day shopper), there was always a risk that she wasn't going to get the absolute best prices. And if she thought that this was a real possibility, she felt exasperated, anxious. She felt as if she was failing herself and her family in some monumental way.

Abbey got back to task. She went through the newspaper flyers and began creating her shopping list. When compelled to do so, she cut coupons from the flyers and paper-clipped them together – from the largest at the bottom of the pile to the smallest at the top. She was close to being finished scrutinizing the flyers that covered almost the entire surface of her ample kitchen table when she began to feel ill at ease. She knew something was not right, but she couldn't put her finger on it. And then, all of the sudden, it hit her – she realized that she was missing one of the flyers that was supposed to come in the mail that Friday morning. "Well," she said, again out loud, "what am I going to do now?"

Daniel had just come through the back door, looked over at Abbey and smiled, "Doing flyer duty again, dear?" he said good naturedly.

Abbey was visibly flustered and her cheeks were taking on a pinkish hue. "It's so frustrating that the darn flyers don't come when they're supposed to," she quipped, "I'm missing a whole flyer for tomorrow's shopping."

Daniel was at the fridge by this time holding a glass under the cold water dispenser. He knew he had to tread carefully where what he thought of as 'the coupon thing' was concerned. "Honey, don't worry about it this week, you can catch up next week," he said matter-of-factly as he made his way back out the door. He chuckled to himself. He just did not understand why Abbey got so worked up over saving a few bucks with store coupons. It's not as if they couldn't afford to pay regular prices or to splurge now and then. He appreciated her efforts at being thrifty, but sometimes she took it much too far. The fact that her coupon-hunting was a mild obsession didn't really bother him; it was the fact that she got so anxious and frustrated that caused concern.

The good thing was that this anxiety and exasperation didn't surface often. He knew that Abbey enjoyed her 'hobby' and was motivated to keep their family expenses in line, and so he left her to it. Once her list was created, and she had her bundle of coupons ready to go, he knew the rest of the evening would be theirs to hang out, visit friends, or just relax by themselves.

Justin – *S u i t c a s e (P a c k i n g) A n x i e t y*

The suitcases were placed side by side on the king-sized bed. Justin was careful to lay an old blanket on top of the duvet before placing them on the bed. Bri didn't want the scuffed, dirty suitcases to soil, or better yet ruin, her off-white linen duvet cover. It wasn't brand new, but it was a wedding gift and she loved it and the way it matched everything else in their bedroom.

The day was finally here. Tomorrow, Bri and Justin were finally heading south for ten days of rest and relaxation. They had chosen an all-inclusive resort on the Riviera Maya, a short drive south of Cancun and close to Playa del Carmen, just a few minutes further south. They were both looking so forward to seeing a bit of Mexico; they had heard many good things about the area around Cancun and neither had ever been to Mexico.

And with the cold, miserable weather they were having, the timing for the trip could not have been more perfect.

It started about two weeks ago. Justin was online surfing the net, looking at shore excursions, restaurants, etc., when he turned to Bri and asked her which bathing suit she was going to pack.

Bri looked at him incredulously and said, "Babe, I'm bringing them all, of course!"

"Babe," he said, "you have six bathing suits. You're not bringing them *all*, are you?"

Bri was just finishing texting her sister. She hit 'send,' stood up, and walked over to Justin, placing her arm around his shoulder. She leaned over and whispered into his ear, "I have to, Babe. I can't leave any of them behind. I need variety. You don't want me wearing the same suit for the entire vacation, do you?" She left the room without waiting for his answer.

Justin looked up from the computer screen and started to feel jittery. Did he need to get another pair of swim trunks? Or two? Justin's packing anxiety was now seeded.

This vacation was exciting and, at the same time, nerve-wracking. On several occasions when he came home from work, he found Bri already home from the office trying on outfits, coordinating colours, and putting things in neat piles in the bedroom. Justin initially thought that Bri 'had it bad': "packing panic," he called it. But he had to admit to himself that he was feeling unsettled; he had absolutely no idea what to pack, or even where to begin. Sure, he knew he had to pack shorts and tee-shirts, but what about other stuff? He didn't want Bri to know that he was getting just as anxious as he thought she was. For her, however, it was just a matter of filling up her suitcase with the items that she had carefully chosen over the past two weeks, reviewing what she had already set aside, and determining what else, if anything, she needed to add.

Bri wanted to get an early start at packing so she had already begun to pile personal items, clothes, etc., on the floor alongside one of the bedroom walls. Now, it was the day before they were to leave, and time to pack. For her, this upfront planning actually gave her a sense of calm that she didn't expect. She was careful to include a couple of warm, rain resistant items just in case the weather turned. She didn't want to be caught without! She knew that she would probably forget something, but it was not going to be the end of the world.

Justin, on the other hand, didn't believe in starting too early, but now he was regretting that decision. It was the day before and he was just starting. He began with some good momentum, packing his swim trunks – all three pairs – his tee-shirts, shorts, a pair of runners and two pairs of sandals. He stopped and looked blankly at the still-empty suitcase. What else should he pack? Did he need long pants? What about dress shirts? He knew that Bri would be packing shampoo, conditioner, etc., but what was he going to need? He could often get away with packing very little for a weekend getaway, but this was for an entire ten days. This was different.

Bri entered the bedroom and made her way over to her suitcase, giving it another once-over. She then looked at Justin's suitcase and smiled up at him. "Everything OK, Babe?" she asked.

Justin turned to her, red in the face. "How is it that you are so calm, and practically finished packing?" he asked of her. He was getting miffed, and she could see it as plain as day. Even though their flight wasn't until 3 pm the next day, it wasn't by chance that they were doing the main part of their packing today. Bri knew that Justin would have some trepidation, and she also wanted to give herself the extra time to be sure she was as thorough as she could be, so she insisted that the suitcases be brought out early.

In a soft voice, Bri said, "Justin, let's do the rest together. I'm going to pack last minute items tomorrow, so let me help you."

Justin looked at her and admitted that he was beginning to second-guess his decisions. He also realized that Bri was so calm and collected because she had done what she could by planning in advance, something that he would definitely do next time! He smiled at his wife, kissed her on the cheek and said, "Let's do this!"

Tom – *L o c k e d C a r A n x i e t y*

He had passed Erica, his assistant, on his way in and greeted her with a "Good Morning." He was in his office now, taking stock of what the day had in store for him. He checked his electronic calendar, logged into his computer and verified that there were no voice messages waiting. It was barely 7:30 am.

Tom sat for a moment while things were still quiet. He chuckled to himself. How many times has he done that in the past few months? Fifteen, twenty, or more? He must be losing it. He wondered if anyone else suffered like he did. Maybe he was over-worked, stressed or maybe he *was* going crazy. For the time being, he put it out of this mind. He had a busy day ahead, and certainly more important things to think about.

Noon came and went as Tom worked his way from meeting to meeting. At 1:15, as he and a group of colleagues were leaving the 7th floor meeting room, he caught up with Jill and asked her if she had time for a quick bite.

She glanced at her watch and said, "Sure, I've got about forty minutes before my next meeting."

Tom looked relieved, and said, "Great. Let's just go to the deli on the main floor to save some time."

They both ordered the soup-and-sandwich special, retrieved their meals from the server, and moved to the cash register. Tom offered to pay, and Jill acquiesced, offering to treat next time. They found a small table in the corner that looked out onto the bustling city street.

Tom waited until they both had a chance to enjoy some of their lunch before he asked, "Jill, can I ask you a silly question?" Jill placed her soup spoon on her side plate and gave Tom an inquisitive look.

"Sure, ask away," she said, maintaining eye contact. She worked with Tom, and respected, admired and really liked him. She wondered what this was all about.

"Do you ever feel that you are one hundred percent sure you have done something, but you second-guess yourself, get anxious, retrace your steps and find that you, indeed, did it?" asked Tom, quite seriously.

Jill looked at him blankly. "You're going to have to give me more than that, Tom," she said, interested.

"OK, so you know that I park my car in that pay lot three blocks down the street – you know the one." Jill nodded affirmatively. "Well," he began, "over the past few months, probably even longer, now that I think about it, I park my car, get out and walk the three blocks to work."

Jill tilted her head, wondering where this was leading. She added, "And so?"

Tom continued, "Well… as I turn the corner and come up John Street, I feel anxious that I didn't lock it… my car, I mean. I know it's irrational and I try to put it out of my mind, but I stop in my tracks. I mean, what if I didn't? I walk towards the car repeatedly pushing the lock button on the remote until I see the car's lights flash. They always do! There was only one time that I can remember that I actually forgot to lock it. Nothing happened, of course, but I always want to make sure it's locked. Am I going crazy? What's going on with me?" Tom took a deep breath and gobbled down another bite of his sandwich.

Jill looked at him, and a smirk began to form at the corner of her mouth. "No, you are not going crazy, Tom," she assured him. "We all do things like that. At least, I do."

Tom couldn't believe what he was hearing. "You do?" he asked.

"Yes," she confirmed. "For me it's not that I fear that I haven't locked my car or my house, but I occasionally get a sick sense that I've left the oven on. That's happened only once, but I occasionally find myself having the same nervous, anxious feeling, especially when I'm no longer at home. And I think to myself, *What if?* You can fill in the possible scenario." She recalled, "One time, I even left a friend's 50th birthday to go and check." Tom looked at her enquiringly. "Yes, Tom, I *had* turned if off!" They both laughed loudly. Tom felt relieved that he wasn't the only one!

"So what do you do to ease the sick feeling you get when you think you've left the oven on?" asked Tom as he finished his last spoonful of soup.

"Well," Jill said, "If I've used the oven, I make a point of double-checking the dials before I leave the house. It's as simple as that. I know that I've checked it, and I can let it go."

Tom wondered if that would work for him. Jill noticed him lost in thought and said, "Just try it, Tom. It can't hurt. Until you can rest assured that just one push of your remote will do it, try starting out with two."

Tom smiled and said, "OK, I'll give it a go."

Jill added, "And don't be so hard on yourself, Tom. Everything these days is electronic. It's no wonder we forget things so easily. It takes no great effort, and locking car doors is no exception. Can you remember when we had to lock our cars *manually* with a key?!"

Nina – *M e n u   A n x i e t y*

As soon as the waiter handed Nina the menu, her heart started pounding. She hadn't yet opened the cover when she began feeling queasy – and in a great restaurant like this one, no less. Luckily, the five friends who joined her for dinner on this beautiful Saturday evening didn't notice anything out of the ordinary. Their eyes were fixated on their own menus, whereas Nina could barely give hers a second glance.

Salvatore's was an excellent restaurant, and she enjoyed eating there. The décor had been described in a local restaurant guide as *rustic Italian renaissance*, complete with wrought iron candelabras and heavy velvet draperies; a wonderful ambience. The service was impeccable, and the food scrumptious.

The problem was the menu. It was far too extensive for Nina's liking. She didn't mind choice when the number of items she had to choose from was relatively few; in fact, the fewer the better, as far as she was concerned. But Salvatore's menu was pages long – it was a veritable catalogue of fine Italian antipastos, soups, salads, pastas, entrées of all sorts, and decadent desserts; if it was Italian, Salvatore's had it on the menu!

She sat almost paralyzed, deep in her own thoughts. She was trying to remember when this apprehension towards restaurant menus had started. More to the point, when was it that her anxiety around making the 'right' menu choice began? She once asked her mother the same thing and her mother responded, "Dear, for as long as I can remember, you always took longer than the rest of us to decide what to eat. Even when you were young and we took you to fast food restaurants," she added, smiling at her daughter. It wasn't anything that anyone took too seriously back then, but as Nina got older, this paralysis became more and more of a nuisance.

The server arrived and his presence startled Nina – as if he had appeared out of thin air. He quickly apologized, and after getting the group's full attention, introduced himself as Andrew and asked if he could start them out with a pre-dinner cocktail. She smiled, embarrassed, and tried to focus on what she wanted to drink. As she was the closest to him, the server tried to make eye contact with her so that she could be the first to order. But Nina did not look up at him. In a low murmur, barely audible, she requested that he start with someone else. That would buy her some time to decide, she thought to herself. That tactic didn't work for long; everyone else knew exactly what they wanted to drink. He took their orders and then turned to Nina. Without even consulting the drink menu she asked for a glass of Chardonnay, which, when the server left to fill the order, she regretted.

This was not starting out to be the fine dining experience she had hoped it would be. She was angry and frustrated with herself, but she wouldn't reveal that to the others. She quickly joined the others in the ongoing conversation about the concert they were all going to attend. Back in the recesses of her consciousness, however, Nina knew she had to look at the menu at some point within the next few minutes… and decide!

A couple of times, during the span of roughly two-and-a-half minutes, Nina thought that Andrew was making his way to their table to take their food orders and she panicked. She finally opened the menu and began her research. Everyone was beginning with a starter. That's not too bad, she thought to herself. She loved Caesar salad and knew it would be a relatively safe bet. It was the main course she was fretting about. Should she have the Penne Arrabiata or the Spaghetti Carbonara? No, she had the Carbonara last time. But boy, it was good! Or, should she go with a meat dish? She heard that the Veal Scallopini was 'to die for,' and Beth, sitting directly across from her, was going to order it. She really should choose something new. Oh, she just couldn't decide!

Trish, who was seated at the far end of the booth, glanced toward Nina and asked, "Have you decided what you're having Nina?"

"Not quite yet," Nina admitted.

"Well, you'd better hurry; Andrew is on his way over," remarked Michelle, gesturing towards Andrew as he approached.

Desperation set in. Nina wanted to be able to order the right thing tonight, with confidence. Andrew arrived and started with Beth this time, thank goodness. A couple of the women asked clarifying questions and decided without much hesitation. Nina smiled to herself, relieved that there were no dinner specials to ponder and worry over.

She was last. It was her turn; she had to decide. A few seconds passed and Andrew asked if he could assist in any way. He was being so nice, Nina thought, but she didn't answer. The others were starting to look her way, and Nina sighed loudly and said, "Oh, I guess I'll go with the Carbonara."

"Excellent choice," said Andrew approvingly as he turned toward the kitchen.

"Yes, we'll see," Nina said under her breath, satisfied that she made a good choice. But was it the *right* choice? If not, she could always come back again!

Caitlyn – *R e t a i l   S a l e s   C l e r k   A n x i e t y*

Oh, not again! This was the third time today. Caitlyn tried to duck behind a rack of sportswear items to avoid making contact with the perky salesperson who had noticed her when she entered the upscale store and who was now bouncing in her direction. As though following a built-in GPS the salesperson found Caitlyn pretending to read the care instructions for a garment that was much too big to fit her small frame.

"Hi, my name is Amy. Can I help you find anything today?" the salesperson chirped.

Caitlyn had to look up. She really didn't want to be rude. "Oh, hi!" she said without making direct eye contact. "No, just looking, thanks!" she added as she moved toward the rack that actually held clothes that were in her size, hoping beyond all hope that Amy would saunter over to another unsuspecting client with money to burn.

"Well, let me just tell you about all of the fantastic sales we have on our outgoing summer stock," Amy continued, unperturbed at Caitlyn's seeming disinterest. Interesting, Caitlyn thought; outgoing summer stock, and it was only the beginning of July.

Amy spent a good three or four minutes rhyming off every last special, discount, and two-for-one promotion that the store was offering at that moment, simultaneously gesturing in multiple directions around the store with flailing arms. Caitlyn was starting to sweat. Her internal voice was taking over; she detested pushy salespeople. They were so obnoxious. She understood that they had to make a living, but did they have to act like vultures? Could they not just say "Good morning," and be on their merry way? Caitlyn knew how to ask for assistance if and when she needed it. She hadn't been in the store for two minutes before she was pounced upon by this poor example of a sincere and genuine store representative. Where did they train these people anyway, at a used car dealership? She smiled. That was it. They were all trained at *Bob & Ted's Used Cars*, out on Highway 24. *Bob & Ted's* had a reputation for its salespeople, and not a good one.

Caitlyn loved shopping: with friends or solo, it didn't matter to her. She enjoyed exploring the new trends in fashion, home décor, and house wares, feeling the textures and fabrics, marvelling at the new colours and styles. And when she invested in herself, she loved it even more. However, what absolutely ruined the experience for her was the anxiety she felt when – not if – she was attacked by the obnoxious, fake or needy sales person who would follow at her heels like a well-trained puppy or a second shadow.

Today, Caitlyn needed, and moreover really wanted, new yoga gear and this store had a fantastic reputation for quality and selection. However, she was beginning to get frustrated and she knew that if things didn't settle down, she'd have to leave and go elsewhere.

She had already been to a competitor in the same shopping complex and had been too exasperated to stay there longer than a few short minutes. In that store, the salesperson's name was Tyrone and he was in his mid-forties, she guessed. The moment he saw Caitlyn enter, his eyes grew to saucer size and he sauntered (it was really more like a sashay) towards her. He greeted her politely with an effervescent, "Hello there", and asked if he could help her find something in her size.

She stopped, smiled politely and looked up at him. "No, thank you. I'm just browsing right now." He made what Caitlyn could only describe as a small 'humph' sound – as if she had personally insulted him – and turned away, yet hovered nearby. The moment she picked up an item, he would say something to the effect of: "That colour would look fabulous on you," or "That would *so* compliment your skin tone." He was on her like flies on flypaper. He was relentless. At first, she got mildly upset and annoyed. But when Tyrone wouldn't back off, she became so full of angst that she couldn't concentrate on what she was doing any longer and had to leave the store. She left the store in a huff, promising herself that she was going to speak to the store manager about Tyrone's overbearing demeanour. That's how she found herself here, in another store, hoping for some peaceful shopping.

Caitlyn stumbled into an oddly placed mannequin that stirred her from her reverie, and apologized to it absent-mindedly. She smiled at herself in embarrassment. She gathered her composure, looked Amy squarely in the eyes and asserted, "Thank you, Amy. I appreciate your assistance, but I'm going to take a few minutes to look through the store myself. When I need your assistance, I will come find you." She quickly turned away, not giving Amy the opportunity to interject.

She felt good. And more important, she felt in control. This was *her* day, and she was glad that she managed to get her retail salesperson anxiety under control.

Cedric – *Visiting Relative Anxiety*

Cedric was seated at the kitchen table drinking his fruit smoothie and writing out a grocery list for the coming week. His partner, Drew, was seated across from him enjoying the last sips of his Americano while glancing through the various sections of the thick Saturday edition of the newspaper.

"C'mon, Drew, give me a hand here," Cedric pleaded, "you're the one who'll be doing most of the cooking anyway."

To that, Drew slowly looked over the top of the newspaper and glowered at Cedric. "They're *your* relatives," he replied, putting undue emphasis on the 'your.'

Cedric let out a somewhat dramatic sigh, and got back to work on the list.

He was actually surprised when Liam, his brother, called a little over a month ago and said that he and his family would like to come for a visit. For a few years now he'd been asking his brother – and his sister-in-law for that matter – to come out west to visit them, with always a "we'll see… someday" in response, so this call came virtually out of nowhere. The next day the travel arrangements were finalized and both Cedric and Drew had managed to secure a week's vacation from their respective employers. Of course, Cedric loved his brother and family, but he really didn't know whether he was up for hosting them for an entire week. Too late now for second-guessing, he deliberated.

Aside from being related by blood, Cedric really didn't have a whole lot in common with Liam. As kids, they had their share of quarrels, arguments and fights, as most siblings do. They were both good in school; Cedric excelled academically while Liam's interests centred on sports. While brothers, they weren't really good friends. Cedric got on well with Natalie, Liam's wife of ten years, and Drew got along fine with both of them as well. The kids were great; Lexy was eight and Lucas was almost seven. They were both very energetic, bright kids.

Cedric was glad that Liam and family were finally making the trek out west. It would be great to see his brother, and marvel at how the kids have grown. Regardless, ever since that initial call, Cedric's stomach was aflutter with butterflies and apprehension, and it got progressively worse as Liam's arrival date approached. Drew was the poster child for 'calm, cool and collected,' and Cedric resented that a bit, which didn't help matters.

A month had passed. Cedric's brother and family were arriving in a few hours. Luckily, the weather promised to be good for the next seven to ten days. Drew and Cedric had already planned several outdoor activities to keep their guests amused, busy, and hopefully, by the end of each day, exhausted. The nearby suspension bridge, an area zip-line course, the local aquarium, and a couple of visits to the beach or a movie or two would keep them occupied while in the city. At their cabin, the guys thought that the kids would enjoy visiting the local First Nations cultural centre, kids' theme park, and a day or two taking it easy at the lake. In terms of things to do, they had the trip in the bag.

Cedric knew that his partner of eighteen years was more concerned with how he was coping than with the actual visit itself. Even though Drew added very little to the grocery list, Cedric knew that he could depend on him for support, encouragement and strength if he needed it. Drew was impossibly easygoing and Cedric knew that if push came to shove, Drew could easily dream up some other activity or diversion to entertain their guests.

That was it! That's one of the reasons why Cedric felt so apprehensive. As far as he could remember, Liam and Natalie were very high maintenance guests. They didn't embark on any adventures of their own; they couldn't make any decisions for themselves, whether it was the type of food they wanted to eat or the kind of activity they wanted to try. They needed to be constantly entertained and led. And, when it came to helping out with dishes, driving, or small chores, Liam just didn't. He was either lazy or possessed no guest etiquette, and truth be told, Natalie was pretty similar. Cedric knew then that he and Drew were going to have to be 'on' 24/7: around-the-clock hosts and tour guides. And this was supposed to be their vacation as well!

Cedric finished his grocery list, placed his smoothie cup in the dishwasher, and sighed.

Drew gathered up the paper and tossed it into the recycling. He looked over at Cedric who was staring out the window and said, "Ric, we're ready. All we have to do is get the groceries. Don't worry. They'll have a great time, and so will we."

Cedric looked at Drew and nodded in agreement, although his heart wasn't really into it. He doubted himself and whether they had made the right plans. Drew noticed his hesitation and added, "Ric, just remember to breathe."

Etta – *Car Wash Anxiety*

The commercials depict the fun-loving young couple washing their car in the driveway of their suburban-esque two-story home. They frolic: splashing and spraying water at each other and tossing soap bubble balls in each others' direction. Inevitably, they finish in a warm embrace in out-of-control laughter.

Etta contemplated this scenario and said out loud, "Ya, right!" She knew better. Inside, she was having a different conversation. What if you have no driveway? No special hose or bucket or sponge? Or, worse yet, no fun-loving partner? What if you have a very dirty, black vehicle – in this case her two-door cabriolet – and it is in dire need of a sponge bath? What if you find yourself putting gas in your tank and before you pay, the pump asks you if you would like to add a car wash to this afternoon's fill-up? It was almost as if her car was crying out to her, "Wash me! Wax me! Love me!"

Etta looked at the pump that waited for her to press the "YES, I'd like a car wash" button and succumb. Etta glanced with trepidation at the dreaded car wash structure and beads of sweat began to trickle down her forehead. She loathed car washes and she had loathed them for as long as she could remember. Mild panic started to set in in the pit of her stomach. "I shouldn't have just eaten," she said to herself, on the verge of tossing her lunch.

The car wash edifice stared back at Etta like a blood-sucking vampire. All she could see were the oversized moving parts. She thought to herself that no brushes should ever be that enormous; soap should never be dispensed from a device that looked like a huge hairbrush on steroids. And what about those giant washing slappers that hit the windshield with the force of a semi truck hitting you head on? And if that weren't enough, wax should never be in liquid form only to be hardened by an oversized hair dryer the force of which could easily propel the car into a vortex, similar to that of a veritable tornado. She remembered Dorothy in *The Wizard of Oz*, and murmured "Toto, we're not in Kansas anymore." She smirked timidly. The car wash represented a different world for Etta, and certainly not Oz.

And that's not the worse part. Etta could probably deal with the mechanics if she were not expected to sit in her car and allow this to take place all around her as she moved at a snail's pace through the temple of car cleanliness doom.

"Not so much," she decided, defending her position.

Lost in this reflection, she found her thoughts wandering into more and more absurd anxiety-inducing scenarios. The soap could seep between the cracks of the car doors and you could risk near-drowning in bubbles that irritate your skin and make you smell like strong minty mouthwash. The gooey wax could get caught in the door parts, forcing you to stay stuck forever in your vehicle, surviving only on banana peels, cold leftover coffee, and the unfinished granola bar that is wedged under the seat. The brushes could lure you into car wash hell where the devil himself is the young pimply teenager who used to be the manager of a fast food joint but has since promoted himself to car wash attendant. Even worse – and because it was more likely – Etta could be so paralyzed with these fears that she would never be able to move her car forward out of the metallic claws that manipulated her through the traumatic encounter to begin with, thus inspiring the car horns and screams of the impatient drivers behind her waiting their turn at the quick Saturday morning 'wash 'n wax.' Worse than any imagined scenario, this real possibility could catapult her into a frenzy of shredded nerves.

Etta hit the "NO, not today" button. Her receipt spewed out at her and she retrieved it, relieved and with her sanity intact. She was glad that she didn't succumb. Did her car wash anxiety win? Yes and no. She was never going to like automatic car washes, but even though she wanted a clean car, she had control.

For the next two hours, Etta drove up and down some of the city's major streets. After all, it *was* a beautiful summer Saturday, and there was bound to be at least one club, association or sports team who was going to be raising money, the safe, manual car wash way.

Owen – *Personal Appearance Anxiety*

B ack in his early high school years, Owen's mother used to hound him constantly about his personal appearance and hygiene. She was always asking him if he remembered to put his deodorant on, if he brushed his teeth, if his underwear was clean. He would just roll his eyes and assure her that everything was cool. He just could not understand why she would get all worked up over his personal business. It's not as if he was a pig, he used to think.

It happened for the first time on opening night of the high school's theatre club production of *Romeo & Juliette*. Owen played Romeo. He learned his lines masterfully, and for an 11th grader, he was a pretty good actor. Dress rehearsal went off without a hitch the night before the opening, which gave everyone connected to the play a needed boost of confidence.

Tonight, the auditorium was packed to the rafters. There were no seats to be had. Moms, dads, sisters and brothers, uncles and aunts, grandparents and friends had all bought tickets to the school's production. There was a bustle in the crowd as the time drew near for the play to begin.

Backstage, the actors were huddled together being given a pep-talk from Mr. Roberts, the theatre arts teacher and director of the play. Everyone could feel the excitement.

"Five minutes to curtain," bellowed Mr. Roberts, notifying everyone to take their places. Owen made a quick detour to the boy's washroom to relieve himself. "Break a leg!" Mr. Roberts shouted to everyone for good luck.

The curtain rose and the play began. The rest, as they say, is history. The moment Owen walked on stage he could hear nothing but uproarious laughter, and saw people gesturing toward him. Sandeep, who played Juliette, pointed down towards his mid-section as nonchalantly as she possibly could. Owen was paralyzed. He didn't even have to look. He knew what people were laughing at. He had forgotten to secure the lace on the flap of his costume's codpiece and it had fallen open, leaving the world to see his shirt flap and orange boxers staring out at them.

Owen was forty now and still suffered from what he called 'personal appearance anxiety.' When he got nervous thinking about an important task, meeting, event or activity – anything that forced him into the public domain – he became giddy, lost focus and often forgot details, like putting on deodorant or brushing his teeth. He had even been known to put on a soiled shirt or dirty socks without the slightest awareness that he had done so, so wrapped up in the activity or event that he could not see the forest for the trees.

The actual anxiety usually didn't set in until he did a mental scan of himself just prior to the activity in question – sometimes too late. When he realized that he may have neglected to put deodorant on, or if his shirt was not clean, he would begin to get nervous: his stomach would clench, and sweat would trickle from the pores on his forehead and under his armpits, which would exacerbate the situation. At that point, he usually could do nothing about it, but the anxiety would cause him more angst.

The being-caught-with-an-open-fly phenomenon surfaced a result of the trepidation and apprehensiveness he experienced immediately before he was to 'perform' or show himself in public. Often, he had to rush to the men's room so that he didn't have to worry about having to 'go' while in the midst of things. Yet, this is where his loss of focus was compounded. Owen frequently forgot to do his fly back up before he left the washroom, which on more than one occasion has made him once again the centre of attention. It had become a vicious circle.

Owen grew a thick skin and could laugh at himself in most situations, which eased the humiliation when he did forget. He was smart enough to observe that his own reaction to the circumstances was the real issue, not the circumstance itself. He knew that the others (friends, colleagues) had moved on and weren't likely to dwell on his idiosyncrasies.

Becca – *G e t t i n g L o s t A n x i e t y*

She was all set to go. She had filled up the gas tank yesterday afternoon on her way home just after she picked the kids up from daycare. Her coffee was stored in the convenient cup holder which was within safe, easy reach. She used the second holder to stow her environment-friendly glass canister of ice-cold water. Her satchel, which contained her files, laptop, and meeting journal, was sitting in the passenger seat beside her, waiting patiently for Becca to get underway.

She even placed her mobile phone in the front pocket of her satchel; she never used it while driving – she didn't need the distraction, and it wasn't legal anyway. It was, however, close enough that, when appropriately stopped, she could access it quickly and without fuss.

Becca had been pursuing this client for a few months now and was excited that she was finally going to meet them in person. It was her 'dream' client, and the work was exactly what inspired her. The only negative thing – the only one – was the fact that this client was located in the valley, and Becca was coming from the city.

The problem wasn't that she disliked driving; she loved it, in fact – if she knew exactly where she was going. The problem was that she was prone to getting lost, and this caused her no shortage of anxiety. It started as soon as she got behind the wheel; she could feel her heart rate increase ever so slightly.

She knew this about herself. It had happened often enough that she always did what she could humanly do to prepare. Aside from arranging her cockpit to facilitate the voyage, today, Becca had three sheets of paper resting on the top of her satchel within easy view. The first was a printed copy of an email message from the client which contained detailed directions to their site from a well-known city landmark. As a back-up plan, she also had both MapQuest and GoogleMaps printouts paper-clipped underneath, which listed street-by-street, turn-by-turn directions. Each contained a map that highlighted (as if in real highlighter marker) the route that she was to follow, the estimated time of the trip, and the number of miles/kilometres it would take to get there. She was prepared.

It still didn't matter. Becca realized early on that if she did not know how to get to a location, whether it be for a client, a restaurant, or a friend's cottage – and she was driving – she left herself extra travel time to compensate if she were to lose her way. Yet, until she actually stepped foot in front of her destination, she was not totally at ease. Preparation was key, but it still didn't alleviate her anxiety... even with the new technology that is available today – GPS included!

Becca manoeuvred her way easily through the city streets as she drove towards the onramp to the highway. This is the easiest way to the valley, isn't it? she wondered to herself. She always second-guessed herself, and her directions, in hope that by chance some entity would intervene and subconsciously present her with a more direct, quicker, easier route. It was too late now. She had made her approach and merged into traffic. Luckily, traffic wasn't bad, because that, too, could be an unwelcomed distraction.

Highway driving was almost therapeutic for Becca. She liked listening to her favourite CDs; meditation; easy-listening, etc., especially when she was on road trips with her family. Today, she had the AM traffic channel playing as it had regular traffic reports that were updated every ten minutes or so. She listened attentively to the reports as she neared the end of the highway portion of her trek. "Construction?" she echoed the radio announcer. "Great, just what I need! I hope they don't detour me," she said to herself as she tightened her grip on the steering wheel while carefully exiting the highway via the off-ramp.

At this point, Becca turned the radio off since she knew it wasn't going to be of any further help, and she needed the calm. Her palms began to sweat mildly as she followed her directions to-the-letter. She was only five or so minutes away from her destination when she noticed the orange construction signs and workers ahead, and slowed down as indicated. "Shoot, a detour!" she exclaimed out loud. She panicked, swallowed a quick swig of water and took a deep breath. I can do this, she assured herself. She followed the other vehicles, praying that they would lead her directly to her new client's offices. And although that was not the case, the detour led her back to the street she was on, and after two more turns, she was pulling into the building's parking tower.

Becca took a deep breath as she parked her car in a stall close to the elevators. Becca has come to terms with this anxiety. It is just a part of who she is. She knows she has a poor sense of direction, and it doesn't make her a bad person. Preparation alleviates a bit of the tension, so she does what she can. And she is OK with knowing that sometimes, that is all she can do.

Sean – *R u d e   P e o p l e   A n x i e t y*

A steady stream of movie-goers was making its way through the pair of heavy glass doors at the entrance to the cinema. The middle-aged guy ahead of Sean pushed the door open with such force that Sean thought it would hit the inside wall and shatter. It didn't shatter, but it did come swinging back at Sean and his date with such backward momentum that it almost pushed Sean back onto the sidewalk. "Idiot," he cursed, "could he have *been* more rude?" He could feel his heart beat a bit faster. "Would it have really taken him any more time to hold the door for us? What is the world coming to? It's just common courtesy," he mumbled under his breath. Rude people – they're everywhere.

They entered the cinema building and got in the queue to purchase their tickets. Sean took a deep breath and settled himself down. He wasn't going to let that neanderthal ruin their evening out.

Thalia, Sean's date, went into the theatre to grab their seats; it was their film's opening night and the theatre was quickly filling up. They didn't want to be caught having to settle for seats in the 'nose-bleed' section. Sean agreed to catch up with her after he stopped off at the concession counter to grab some popcorn and soft-drinks. Sean waited patiently in line – he was third from the front, and was relieved to know that it wouldn't take long to be served. There were three concession attendants serving the public with another three acting as back-up support. All six, he imagined, were high school students working to support their teenaged needs and wants, and benefit from free passes to a summer that promised to be full of good blockbuster movies.

As he was looking around the lobby, shifting his gaze from one 'Coming Attraction' movie poster to another, he noticed two teen-aged girls, probably 13 or 14 years of age, coyly butting their way into one of the other lines. By now, the lines were eight to ten people deep, and the wait was pushing ten minutes. The girls were cutting in line in front of a pair of elderly women, who were now fourth in line from the front. The women looked at each other as if expecting the other one to intervene in some way. Instead, they just shook their heads and allowed this contravention of queue protocol to transpire.

Sean was peeved, and was not as willing to overlook the girls' transgression. He thought it was just plain rude and disrespectful for these two young people to take advantage of these two unsuspecting women, who were, no doubt, out on the town for some honest entertainment. He could feel his jaw clenching, as it often did when he came across examples of social insolence. Sean was guided by his strong values and moral code and he believed that everyone should be treated fairly, justly and respectfully, regardless of the situation.

He leaned as far out of his line as he could without losing his spot altogether. After all, he wanted to get his popcorn before his movie started. He managed to catch the attention of one of the young girls by saying, "Excuse me; I believe that the end of the line is back there," as he made an exaggerated gesture to the back of the line.

The young girl quickly turned her back on Sean and stared at her girlfriend, silently pleading for some sort of back up support. The other girl just smiled and looked ahead, trying to ignore the situation altogether.

Gaining some resolve, one of the elderly women came to Sean's aid by lightly placing her index finger on the shoulder of the girl who had turned her back on Sean and added, "This gentleman is right, young lady. We all have to wait our turn."

The girl farthest from Sean rolled her eyes and tugged on the sleeve of her friend and sauntered with her in tow to the back of the line, which was now twelve people deep.

"Serves them right," Sean said with smirk on this face.

"Thank you," the elderly women expressed simultaneously. "It's nice to know that all young ones aren't like that," one of them added. Sean nodded his agreement, and returned to face the concession. He was now the next person to be served. He wondered... His concession attendant's name was Rocky. After placing his order, Rocky's helper filled the soft drink cups while Rocky filled the bucket with popcorn. Passing the snacks to Sean, Rocky stated, "That's $16.95."

Sean made a point of waiting for the 'please'. Time was pushing on, and he didn't want to keep Thalia waiting so he quickly handed Rocky a $20 bill and waited for the change.

Without saying a word, Rocky handed Sean his change, and uttered, "Next in line!" Sean just shook his head, muttered something about 'parents', and crossed the lobby to the theatre.

Kai – *P a s s e n g e r   A n x i e t y*

K ai grabbed onto the armrest between him and the passenger on his right, without realizing that the other passenger – a male in his mid-thirties – was already comfortably leaning on it to support the book he was holding in his left hand. Kai, embarrassed, smiled to the man apologetically. He didn't like turbulence and his first instinct was to grab for the armrest. Both armrests, actually.

Kai's neighbour on the plane could tell that the recent shudder had made Kai nervous. The man turned to Kai and said matter-of-factly, "That was just a bump. We're safe."

Kai appreciated the guy's attempt to relieve him of his apprehension. "Yeah, I guess," he said. "I've just never become comfortable flying." He gathered his thoughts and resumed the rationalization for his faux pas: "You know, if you think about it, we don't have any control over what happens to us up here. We are in this long metallic tube, 39,000 feet above terra firma, hurtling through the heavens at a rate of 450 miles per hour, all at the mercy of two guys who, as luck would have it (or not have it), are the only mortals who can see where we are going."

The man beside him chuckled and nodded his agreement, "You're not too far off there, my friend," he said calmingly. "My name's Kyle, by the way," he said, extending his hand.

Kai took the man's hand: "Kai." he added.

They continued the idle chit-chat for the next quarter of an hour. When the flight attendants passed by with airline-issued headphones, they both opted to take advantage of the in-flight entertainment. Kyle chose a feature length film while Kai wavered and then settled on the audio entertainment. He wanted to drown out the sound of the jet engines with some relaxing music. It seemed to work, at least for the time being.

Kai listened to the music. Lulled by the subtle tones of the spa channel, he began reflecting on his concern about flying. He wondered whether his angst was about flying at all, or whether flying was just another context that manifested the anxiety? He mentally formulated a list of all of the modes of transportation that he frequently used. He carefully considered each one in turn. It didn't take him long to come to the conclusion that he didn't get anxious about flying, per se; he became anxious when he was forced into the position of being a *passenger*. Ah-Ha! A revelation! This was a significant turning point, he thought, in his ability to respond to, or lessen, the anxiety.

He contemplated further. It was all about control, or the lack of control. Passengers very rarely had control; at least, he'd never come across a situation in which, as a passenger, he'd had the opportunity to be in complete control. He thought back to a couple of the most recent trips he had made as a passenger, and details began to fall in place.

He remembered a situation that occurred just two weeks ago with a close friend of his, Netika. They had made reservations at this well-known restaurant up the coast that was situated on a promontory with a magnificent view of the ocean. Netika drove. In retrospect, he laughed to himself, this was the first obvious clue that he was not in control.

They navigated their way successfully through the city streets to the double-lane highway that was going to lead them to their fine dining experience. Kai had his eyes peeled for anything that he thought Netika might not see; other cars, pedestrians, dogs, stop lights. At one point, she looked sideways at him and declared, "No back seat drivers in this vehicle, please!" Kai ignored her sarcasm and continued providing his assistance – it was his only way to have some input.

At one point, Netika had to suddenly brake, and as she did, so did Kai. His leg almost went through the floor; pain shot through his foot right up through his hip. They stopped in plenty of time to avoid smacking the car in front of them, but Kai was not impressed. And he was humiliated! He was a nervous wreck until they were finally seated at their table overlooking the ocean, a cold beer in his hand.

He thought of motorcycles. He couldn't remember ever driving one himself, let alone being a passenger. And that would just never happen. Not in his lifetime, he thought to himself. Trains. What about trains or subways? He didn't travel by train often enough to consider them seriously; however, he'd used the occasional subway car, and weren't they basically the same thing? Hundreds of people jammed into a moving torpedo run by computer, and no one physically in control.

Kai quickly turned to thinking about all of the scientific principles and measures surrounding travel… things like the physics of flight; statistics on the likelihood of plane crashes; the relatively small number of traffic fatalities compared to the total number of vehicles on the road, etc. The math and science behind these things made them seem less unpredictable, less frightening. Over time, Kai believed that reminding himself of these and other simple truths would allow him to ease his tension and anxiety and actually enjoy his passenger status, free from the potential stressors of being in control.

Hoight – *Travel (Into the Unknown) Anxiety*

It's not the flying in an airplane that make me anxious," responded Hoight to the person sitting beside him, "it's... well... it's flying into the unknown. You know, a strange city or a foreign country. I just feel so out of place and disoriented."

The young woman sitting beside Hoight smiled sympathetically as she listened to Hoight's explanation. A few moments prior, she had noticed that Hoight's right leg was vibrating at an impossible rate. In fact, it was vibrating so much that she could feel it herself and it was becoming irritating. She wondered now whether it was a good idea that she had asked Hoight if he was nervous about flying, because clearly, he was nervous about *something*.

Hoight continued, "On the one hand, I love travelling and experiencing new things. You know... the food, the people, the culture. But I seem to get very nervous about halfway through a flight – or even on a train – about what lies in store for me once I get to my destination. Kinda' stupid, huh?" he asked, giving the young woman a sideways glance.

"Well," she began, "I love to travel and travelling into the unknown is one of the aspects that I love the most. Different people, new places, not knowing exactly what awaits you; it's all rather exciting to me." She stopped there. She didn't want to give Hoight the impression that she thought he was crazy. Although she did wonder why, if travelling caused him so much trepidation, he would put himself though such torture. She noticed that he was now fidgeting with the pen that he used to fill out his customs declaration card and wondered if her words had put him on edge. Before she could say anything to lessen the impact of her last statement, Hoight continued.

"You mean to say that you don't get at least a bit apprehensive that things aren't going to work out or that you'll arrive and not know what to do next or that no one will understand you?" Hoight went on, working himself into a bit of a state. "I mean, even in our own country, things can be so different. Everything seems so strange, sometimes even bizarre. Take New York City, for example. How can anyone who doesn't live there possibly survive? Millions of people doing millions of things; the noise; the hustle! How do you people deal with it? How do you stay calm knowing that so many different things can happen?"

Lucky that we aren't heading to New York! the young woman thought to herself, feeling bad for Hoight. She really didn't know how to settle him down or where to take the conversation. He turned to stare out the window, which gave her a few moments to think.

The young woman was interested in Hoight's angst; she thought it was unique. She wondered what the root of the anxiety might be. Obviously, he enjoyed travel; he had said as much. But what was it that was causing him such apprehension? Perhaps it was the fact that he was putting himself into situations that were outside of his comfort zone; situations in which he perceived he had no control. This was interesting. She had always been led to believe (and believed herself) that moving out of one's comfort zone was a good thing... that we learned more, experienced more.

The young woman experienced a sudden sense of déjà vu. She was momentarily taken back to a class she had taken in college. She remembered a model that a professor had once presented that was used within the context of learning. The model illustrated the movement from our 'comfort zone' to the 'learning zone' and then to the 'panic zone'. She remembered the prof stating that it was important that everyone should, at times in their lives, progress to the 'learning zone,' because it was within this zone that true learning and transformation would occur. He also asserted, she remembered, that it was not his intent to force his students into the 'panic zone,' since in this zone the focus was no longer on the learning, but on survival. She learned that living in our comfort zone without experiencing the 'learning zone' would make for a pretty boring life. So, how could she pass this knowledge on to this man sitting beside her in a way that would serve him? She remembered that the key to being in the learning zone was to be open to new things, and take action.

"You know what helps me when I put myself into new situations, regardless of what they are?" she finally asked Hoight in a soft, yet determined voice. She didn't wait for an answer. "I take action. I take a deep breath, and get right to it."

She noticed that Hoight appeared interested, and continued: "When I'm out of my comfort zone, I take control of the situation, because, let's face it, we have control over much more than we think we do. Using New York, for example, where there is no language barrier, except for the strong accent," she said, and winked at Hoight, "I'd get in a cab, make my way to my hotel, get a map of the area and set out on foot to acclimatize myself to my surroundings. This way, I put myself in control of the situation. In fact, I do this in any city I travel to. I follow this same routine which really helps me get my bearings which, in turn, gives me a real sense of calm and excitement at the same time. As I said, it puts *me* in control."

"That's just it," Hoight agreed. "I feel as though I'm out of my comfort zone and that I don't have control. But what you're saying is that I do. I *do* have control. I can see that." Hoight pondered for a couple of moments. He appeared less jittery and began to settle down a bit. "It's about motivating myself to take action so that I have control."

"Absolutely!" the young woman said supportively. "Now, that's not to say that stuff won't happen, but if you are in control, you will learn how to deal with it."

The captain announced that they would be landing in Montreal in twenty minutes. Hoight took a deep breath, glanced beside him and smiled at the young woman. "Well," he said, "there's no time like the present."

Jaclyn – *M e e t i n g   N e w   P e o p l e   A n x i e t y*

In the end, Jaclyn was glad that she went. Her colleagues at the office had suggested that she become a member of the newly-formed professional association so that she could meet new people, network, and learn from others who shared her work and professional interests. Prior to joining, however, she decided that she would attend a meeting to determine whether it was going to work for her or not.

She wasn't disappointed. The people seated at her table seemed genuine and she actually managed to have a couple of interesting conversations. The topic of the evening was relevant and timely and the presenter was both entertaining and informative. During the break, business cards were circulated without the awkward promise of follow-up telephone calls or 'let's get together for coffee' pledges. The evening ended on time and Jaclyn lingered to thank the guest speaker and say good-bye to a handful of new acquaintances. So it had gone well in the end.

On her way to the meeting location, however, Jaclyn was feeling very nervous and resentful for having made the commitment to attend. The thought of belonging to the professional association and reaping the benefits of the continuing education sessions seemed useful in and of themselves, yet the fact that all of this centred around her having to meet new people put her on edge.

Jaclyn always felt anxious meeting new people, whether in a purely social situation or for business. She always felt as though she was under pressure to make a good first impression while, at the same time, feeling as though she wouldn't cut it: that she wouldn't connect well with the new group or that she wouldn't make the most of the opportunity even if it were staring her in the face. She knew as well that her anxiety often manifested outward in certain observable behaviours, making things worse so that she would start worrying about triggering a messy downward spiral which would just compound the situation even more.

Jaclyn often experienced this seemingly interminable instant: hyper-aware of the need for a split-second intervention that would make her compelling to others and in complete control of the situation. To her, the question was always: "Will I be able to press my own ON button in time?" in the precise moment that would rescue her from the clutches of her own insecurity, and catapult her to self confidence and articulacy.

Emotionally, Jaclyn became fearful, despondent, disdainfully amused and embarrassed at the bottomless pit of her own insecurity. She would feel inadequate, needy and resentful of the fact that the 'others,' as she thought of them in these moments, had the balance of power in these new situations – at least according to Jaclyn – especially if they seemed confident or self-assured. She would experience a crushing nervousness in her own mind over whether she would be able to pull off the now-dreaded exchange and create a successful end; a nervousness over whether she would be able to steer her way through her discomfort to a sense of composure and conversational ease.

Physically, she would first experience an intense pressure in her upper gut, followed by a panicky feeling of wanting to flee from the situation altogether. Her heart would race, her hands would tremble and become sweaty, and her soft, pale complexion would become flushed and rosy in colour. And she knew that people would notice, aggravating the situation even more.

Jaclyn was nearing her destination with only a few minutes to go. Her emotional and physical states had taken over and, she laughed ruefully to herself, she was exhausted just thinking about how complicated this whole sharing-of-the-planet thing could be. Despite – or strengthened by – her sense of humour, Jaclyn had to face her fears: this wasn't the first, nor would it be the last time, she would meet new people.

She settled into her parking stall, turned off the engine and began her regimen. She took in several long, even breaths. She began to engage in simple meditation and engaged in positive self-talk where she put the situation into perspective. This time, the fact was that she had as much right as everyone else to be there; she was as competent, amiable and intelligent as other members or new guests; and she had something of value to offer. This was her first time there, so she would be treated with kindness and respect. She reminded herself that 'they' were just human, not divine beings, and that if she didn't connect with anyone, it would not be the end of the world. Worst case scenario: it would not be the first or last awkward encounter she would ever experience. Best case scenario: she would actually become fast friends or co-conspirators with one or two of the attendees. With this, she got out of her car and made her way to the elevator that would transport her to the room filled with interesting new people who were eager to make her acquaintance.

Matthew – *U r i n a l   A n x i e t y*

Large velvet drapes swung down from the rafters, concealing the stage while the house lights gently illuminated the theatre. Finally, the intermission. The professional theatre company's adaptation of Agatha' Christie's *Ten Little Indians* was well done, yet the intermission was long overdue. Legs needed to be stretched, wine needed to be drunk, and Matthew needed to use the facilities – badly. He had made the mistake of drinking several glasses of water, as well as two glasses of wine, during the group's pre-theatre dinner.

Matthew left the rest of the group in the lobby where they congregated during the intermission to enjoy another glass of wine or a piece of Belgian chocolate, and quickly made his way to the men's washroom. Since the bathroom was small and the first act had been a long one, he wondered if he was fast enough to beat the onslaught of men racing to use one of the few urinals or cubicles stationed in the small lavatory.

He turned the corner and saw the group of men standing just outside the washroom door. He was too late. He began to feel a sense of dread in the pit of his stomach. Matthew prayed that everything would be fine, knowing realistically that it was more than just possible he would have a problem.

His need to use the washroom bordered on desperation. He knew others were in the same boat. That sense of commonality that would bind lesser men into a false sense of brotherhood didn't alleviate his impending anxiety. He managed to engage in some trivial small-talk with the guy in front of him to take his mind off his fear, which made the wait at least a little less tedious.

The intermission was only twenty minutes long, and he had been in line for ten of those minutes. The line moved steadily, but just not quickly enough. By the time Matthew had reached the bathroom door, he had begun praying to his bladder god for another few moments.

He was next in line. At that moment, panic set in. He noticed that the urinals were set close together and that they didn't have any dividers to separate them. Oh... My... God! he said to himself under his breath. Could this situation be any worse? He did a quick search for the washroom's cubicles and found three to his right. All were occupied. Crap! he thought to himself, and no pun intended! When he reached this level of urgency, Matthew made a point to wait for a cubical where he could relax and let things flow at their own pace. Tonight, it was different. He didn't have the time to wait for a cubical. But with no dividers? This was going to be an exercise in futility, he thought to himself –

inadvertently predicting, and thus inviting, his urinal anxiety to rule his life once again.

Matthew quickly stepped up to the awaiting urinal. He unzipped his fly, got ready and waited. Nothing happened. He could sense the men still in line, each with their eyes boring a hole in the back of his head. Could they tell nothing was happening? He became more and more anxious at his inability to perform. Contritely, he mused over this whole new meaning to 'performance anxiety.' Matthew stared blankly at the wall in front of him, pleading with his bladder god to *do* something. He dared not turn his head to see if the other men were looking at him, judging him. He tried to concentrate on the colour of the tile, the pattern, the grout – anything to take his mind off what he was supposed to be doing, but couldn't. Nothing came forth. Nothing! What should he do? This was mortifying. He not only had to go like a race horse, but he was so embarrassed that he couldn't even think straight.

Suddenly, a cubical door opened and an elderly gentleman came out to wash his hands before making his way back out to the lobby. As Matthew was just about to turn to bolt into the cubical, a teenager scooted in before him, leaving Matthew stranded in the middle of the room. He not only lost the opportunity to use the cubical, but in so doing, he gave up his place at the urinal. It seemed at this very moment that his bladder god wasn't answering his prayers because he felt that at any second, the dam that was his bladder was going to erupt, releasing a torrent; a flood the likes of which no washroom had ever before seen.

Matthew burst out of the washroom in a flurry. He just happened to notice the disabled person's washroom sign as he hurried from the men's. He also noticed that the lock indicated "vacant." He scurried into the disabled person's washroom, bolted the door, whipped down his pants, sat down on the toilet (forgetting to put the tissue paper cut-out on the seat), took a deep breath and relaxed. It seemed to take forever. He realized he was somewhat detached from reality when he heard a voice announce that the play was going to recommence. Matthew arranged his affairs, washed up, and checked himself in the mirror.

He joined his group as they were just about to re-enter the theatre. A couple of his friends inquired about his wellbeing, and were met with Matthew's assurance that all was well. His partner looked at him and asked, "Happened again?" to which Matthew just nodded and proceeded to take his seat.

Quinn – 'Cop' Anxiety

Quinn was at the wheel. She and three of her girlfriends had booked a four-door sedan from their neighbourhood's car share program and were heading out of the city for a 'girl's weekend' away. They were prepared. The trunk carried their duffle bags and suitcases and the car's drink holders held lattes and other drinks *du jour* to get them started on their way. Of course, they had stocked up on croissants and other goodies to give them sustenance for at least the first hour or so.

Getting out of the city was always a pain, especially on the Friday before a long weekend, but the girls managed to load up the car, stop for coffee and get on the road at a reasonable time. As they made their way to the highway on-ramp, Quinn checked the clock on the dash and it read 9:38 am.

The highway was slow going. Slower than usual, Quinn thought to herself, gripping the steering wheel with a bit more vitality. The four young women were discussing what their first order of business would be when they arrived at their coastal motel. Everyone was upbeat and in a fantastic mood, and the conversation led to deciding whether lounging on the beach or doing a bit of shopping would be first on their list.

As Quinn steered the car around a bend in the highway, she noticed that traffic was coming to a halt. She began to feel sick to her stomach because she knew that this could mean only one of two things; construction or cops. She began to distance herself from the conversation in a way that was distinctly noticeable to her three car mates.

"It's probably just construction, Q," suggested Carly in a very light-hearted, noncommittal voice. She was seated in the passenger seat next to Quinn and she turned ever-so-slightly and winked at her two friends in the back seat. The meaning of the wink was implicit; they all knew of Quinn's unconditional, yet unjustifiable, fear of police officers.

Quinn barely heard Carly, but smiled subtly while focusing all of her attention on the situation ahead. And then she saw it: the flashing of the blue and red lights that confirmed her worst possible nightmare – the presence of cops!

"Oh God," she sighed out loud, "what's going on?"

The other three became silent as Carly reached over to turn the radio down. All four women were now peering out of the windshield to try to figure out what was going on ahead of them.

"I don't think it's an accident," said Carly as she scoured the horizon.

"I just think it's a belt check," said Tanya from the back seat. "I heard on the radio that they were going to be doing random checks all over the city this weekend."

Quinn's forehead began to perspire and her hands were becoming sweaty. She gripped the steering wheel as if she were sitting in the front seat of a corkscrew roller coaster ride and holding on for dear life. She did *not* like cops. She became worked up and tense when they were anywhere within her vicinity. She couldn't explain it, to herself or her friends or family. For some reason, she always felt that cops had a personal vendetta against her; that she was the guilty one even though she had done absolutely nothing to warrant that reaction.

Carly reached over and gently placed her left hand on Quinn's shoulder. Despite the lightness of her touch, Quinn flinched. Carly said, "Quinn, we're wearing our seatbelts. Everything will be fine."

Quinn withdrew into her thoughts. Calm down, Quinn, she thought, feeling embarrassed and silly. This has happened before, she told herself. You always get through it. She remembered another instance that occurred a few months prior when a police woman had come into her office looking for a colleague who was witness to a fender-bender that had happened that morning. The sudden arrival of the female cop had taken Quinn so off-guard that she thought she was going to faint. The cop approached Quinn's desk and politely asked to speak with the person in question. Quinn remembered hesitating, fearing inexplicably that the cop was there to cuff her and throw her into the slammer. She stared vacantly at the police woman while this scenario played over and over in her consciousness. After a few uncomfortable moments, the cop cleared her throat, forcing Quinn to come back to reality. Well, I guess she's not here to arrest me, Quinn thought to herself as she offered to escort the woman in uniform to her colleague's office.

By this time, the cop – a police*man* this time – was checking the seat belts of the inhabitants of the car two ahead of theirs. Quinn took a deep breath, sighed and turned to the others and said, "All buckled up?"

Quinn's hands were still clenched around the steering wheel as she pressed her foot on the pedal, leaving the cop behind. Her heart rate, on the other hand, had begun to return to normal and her forehead was shiny but not dripping as before. Quinn knew it was silly, but she couldn't help it; cops upset her, and they probably always would. The conversation had started up again and the light-hearted atmosphere in the car was beginning to return. She once again looked forward to the drive ahead.

Karen – *Hot Flash Anxiety*

K aren and Gwen – two of my esteemed colleagues – were already in the midst of a penetrating conversation when they entered the lunchroom. I looked up to grab their attention and to ask if they wanted to join me, but stopped myself as I heard a defining snippet of their conversation; clearly they were talking 'menopause.' Both were so fixated on the other and their conversation that they did not, luckily, notice me. They grabbed their lunches and sat at the table directly behind mine.

Now, I am not one to eavesdrop into conversations – even the most riveting. However, anyone who was seated in the lunch room could have easily been a captivated member of their audience. Lunchroom chats were fair game!

"But it is so embarrassing," said Karen as she crossed to the microwave to heat up her leftovers.

"I know, Karen," agreed Gwen, who was already seated at their table.

Karen continued, not hearing Gwen. "I couldn't believe it happened in the middle of my presentation this morning. And not just any presentation – to Globacon! We've been trying to get their account for ages and here I am, presenting the benefits of partnering with us, when I start to get really flushed. It's as if someone from the *Starship Enterprise* instantly transported me to *the* most humid spot on earth." Gwen nodded, taking a bite of her sandwich, while Karen retrieved her meal and headed back to the table.

"You know what I'm talking about," she asserted, looking squarely at Gwen. "I could feel my face flush – physically flush – and no doubt turn the deepest shades of red possible. And if that weren't all, a moment later, I could feel trickles of sweat pour down from my temples and from the back of my neck." She took a breath. "Quelle horreur," she exclaimed in mock French, shaking her head as if to remove the experience from memory. "It only lasted for a few moments, but I'm sure people thought I was having a fit or something. And the fact that I knew what was happening made it even worse. I got so anxious that I'm sure I neglected to cover some important details."

Gwen took another bite of her sandwich before she continued. "I still get them too, but not as much anymore. I guess I'm getting over it, thank goodness," admitted Gwen.

"Yes, but surely you've never dealt with it in front of a prospective client and your colleagues," added Karen.

"You'd be surprised, Karen," Gwen said. "Get this: the very first time it happened to me was when I was interviewing for this job." Karen looked up from her meal and stared blankly at Gwen.

"You're kidding!" she exclaimed.

"God's honest truth," she whispered as she crossed her heart with a gesture of her right hand. "Of course, I was dealing with an already stressful situation – an interview. And I really wanted the job, so I was doubly stressed. Had I known that stress may often trigger a hot flash episode, I may have handled it better, but this was the first time. So I was…"

"Wait, wait," Karen interrupted Gwen. "Hold on, what do you mean that stress triggers hot flashes?"

Gwen put up her hand as if she was a traffic cop halting an oncoming bus, "I'll get to that, but I want to finish my story. So, where was I? Right, I was sitting across from Dunbar, Gail and Peggy in the conference room when all of the sudden my whole body got really hot, and my face began to feel really warm. Luckily, they had offered me a glass of water when I entered the room, so I took a sip. Looking back, it was kind of funny. Peggy handed me a tissue and indicated for me to wipe my forehead. She had asked me if I felt ill, and I really didn't. She was so concerned. I told her that I was just a bit nervous. I mean I wasn't stupid – I knew I was approaching the time, but it didn't sink in at that particular moment. Boy, what an encounter. Suffice it to say, my little episode did nothing to stop them from hiring me, so I don't think you have anything to worry about with Globacon. They're professionals, you're professional. And it's not the last time they'll be meeting with you, is it?" Gwen asked, shifting her eyes to her apple.

"Well, no," admitted Karen. "I guess you're right." Remembering Gwen's earlier comment, Karen piped up again, "Gwen, what did you mean that anxiety can trigger hot flashes?"

Gwen met Karen's eyes and began, "Oh right. Well, I guess when menopausal women get into stressful situations, or get worried over something, this state of anxiety may bring on an episode."

"So, can anything be done, you know, to avoid it?" asked Karen.

"Not avoid *per se*, but you know what I do? I declare it." Gwen said proudly.

"Declare it? What the heck does that mean?" quipped Karen.

Gwen smiled and continued, "Karen, I simply declare that I am having a hot flash and to please bear with me. It's as simple as that. Menopause is not a societal faux pas, so I don't treat it like one. It really helps. And it helps when I'm preparing for a situation that may cause some anxiety – for example, my first date two months ago with Tony. I had a hot flash during dinner, so I declared that it was happening, and we went on from there. No biggie. I even joke about it sometimes. By the way, I'm seeing him tomorrow night." Gwen winked at Karen and she smirked back.

Needless to say, I learned a bit about hot flashes during that lunch hour, not that – being a guy – I'll ever need the info personally!

Harry – *O p e n i n g   B i l l s   A n x i e t y*

They were sitting there, all of them, in a neat little pile on the corner of the kitchen counter. He didn't know why he saved them for the end of the week, but he did. And it was the same thing week in and week out.

When Harry came home each day from his tech support job, he would park in the underground parking lot, ride the elevator to the main level, retrieve his mail, discard the junk mail, and proceed to his modest seventh floor, one-bedroom apartment. Upon entering, he typically greeted his four-year old cat, Furball – if she wasn't playing 'hide and seek' – and walked through to the kitchen to sort his mail. It wasn't very often that items of great interest came through standard post, however, when it did happen, he set the items aside to look at later and deposited the bills and financial statements in a pile on the corner of the kitchen counter that was used for the exclusive purpose of stockpiling what he referred to as his 'formal correspondence.'

It was Friday, and the end of the week. And although Harry set aside this time every Friday, just before dinner or getting together with his friends for a night on the town, he could feel his pulse race as he ventured toward his pile of statements and bills. He put his hand around the pile of stuffed envelopes and lifted them off the counter with a growing sense of imminent doom.

What have I spent? he thought to himself as he moved to his usual work space at the dining room table. How much do I owe? How much money do I have in my accounts? Do I have enough to cover my bills? What will my financial statements tell me? Have I lost money on my investments? All of these internal questions added to Harry's anxiety. If he didn't have high blood pressure at any other time during the week, he certainly did Friday evenings.

As a way to alleviate some of the stress associated with this weekly chore, he further separated his pile into two categories: Bills and Statements. Luckily this week, Harry had only one financial statement in the pile. However, what he soon came to realize was that the other pile, numbering seven envelopes, contained mostly bills. He couldn't figure out whether this was a positive thing or a negative one. This lack of certainty caused further consternation. Man, he thought to himself, why do I do this to myself? This is ridiculous! Get on with it, dude!

As he began to tear open the envelope that held the financial statement, he paused for a moment, quickly wiping the sweat that had accumulated on his palms onto his jeans. He scanned the document, his hands mildly shaking. It was two pages in length, as usual, and as he finally reached the bottom of the second page, he found himself breathing a huge sigh of relief. His investments had paid off. At this, his pulse began to slow down a bit. I should start with the financial statements every week, he thought to himself, remembering that he had received similar news from his last two statements. This awareness gave Harry a renewed sense of confidence and a boost of positive energy. He placed the statement to his left for filing, and reached for his first bill.

He noticed from the envelope that the first bill in the pile was from one of his credit cards. He made a snap decision to sort his bills. In one pile he placed his monthly bills, such as utilities or insurance. In the other he placed his credit card, gas, and cell phone bills. Of course, the rationale for doing this was that the utilities and insurance bills were pretty fixed in their amounts, whereas his credit card, gas and cell phone bills were always different, and sometimes frightfully so. He wanted to deal with them last.

Harry proceeded to open his utility bills: water, hydro, gas, etc. He experienced some initial tension due to increases in each of these utilities until he realized that it was because they reflected the fact that they were in the dead of winter. No real surprises then, he reflected further.

Now onto the other bills, he told himself. Harry really couldn't remember his spending habits over the past few weeks but had a sick feeling that they weren't very good. One after the other, he opened each of the remaining bills. Only one really threw him for a loop. Not that he didn't agree with the bill. In fact, he knew that it was correct. Just to be sure, however, he reconciled his receipts to the bill in question. Correct, as initially thought. I have to be more careful, he thought to himself, remembering his spontaneous purchase of new ski boots. He felt guilty as he realized – much as he had in the store – that his current boots were just fine.

Well, not so bad after all, everything considered, he admitted to himself as he gathered up the torn envelopes and threw them into the recycle bin. He powered up his laptop and proceeded to pay most of his bills. Those he couldn't pay online, he would write a cheque for on Sunday and get in the mail on Monday.

Harry knew that he couldn't really do anything to alleviate the anxiety associated with his bills and statements, aside from being more mindful of his spending habits and, of course, just not letting the uncertainty get the best of him. He smiled to himself: well, at least not for another week.

Sonya – *W h e r e   d o   W e   S i t ?   A n x i e t y*

Richard opened the large oak door to the restaurant, allowing the five other members of the party to enter before him.

"Always the perfect gentleman," declared Louisa.

Now actually at the restaurant, Sonya was beginning to tense up. She had never been to this restaurant. It had opened about a year ago to rave reviews and she had been looking forward to the experience for some time. It was not an expensive restaurant, per se, just one that people were talking about, and it was difficult to secure a reservation without weeks of advance notice.

Sonya agreed with Louisa as she passed Richard at the door. She gave him a quick smile, and he winked at her knowingly. Even though they had made reservations, the eight o'clock rush of patrons was gathered at the host station leaving names and requesting view seating. While distinct conversations were inaudible, the overall rumbling of voices and sounds was overwhelming.

The crowd of people didn't help matters any. Even at the best of times, when Sonya was by herself, she felt utterly stupid and embarrassed as a result of her 'little issue,' as she called it. Now, she would be exposing herself to a restaurant full of complete strangers. She took a deep breath and followed the others into the lounge, which was separated from the dining room by the restaurant's massive bar. Great, she thought to herself; I can't even get the lay of the land before they seat us.

Sonya ordered a glass of Pinot Gris, took a couple of sips, and settled into the comfy lounge chair knowing that the lounge wait, at least, was temporary. It had been a busy week for everyone, so they all had a cocktail to unwind before dinner. The conversation was lively and relaxed, as it often was with the six of them. The small group enjoyed each other's company for a good twenty minutes before the host returned.

"Your table is ready now," he quietly announced to the group. Richard's eyes met Sonya's. She finished the few drops left in her glass and allowed Richard to help her out of her seat. Richard indicated that Sonya should take the lead, with the other four following closely behind. Sonya followed the host into the main dining room. As she approached the tastefully designed room, she began to feel queasy. She reached for Richard's arm, and he offered it without hesitation. Sonya immediately noticed where the host was heading and she froze on the spot. He was heading toward a table that was situated virtually in the centre of the large dining room. Even before he noticed Sonya's grasp tighten on his arm, Richard knew this would not do. She gave him a quick glance, and he stepped up to the plate.

"Excuse me: Alexander, is it?" Richard asked, getting the attention of the host just as they were arriving at the table. "May we try another table?" Sonya let out a sigh of relief, but she knew her predicament wasn't over quite yet. The others were barely disrupted at the confusion, still deep in catching up on the week's events.

"Well… yes, I guess," responded Alexander. "We haven't seated the other two parties yet. How about this lovely spot here, close to the window?" He indicated another table close to the one beside which they were currently hovering.

Sonya, feeling even further trepidation about the thought of being seated at the second table option, exclaimed, "What about that booth in the corner with the curving banquette? That looks perfect." Sonya started toward the table before waiting for a response from Alexander.

Leaving the restaurant, the six members of the small group said their goodbyes and parted ways. Richard had parked at Sonya's place so he escorted her home. It was a pleasant evening and perfect for a twenty minute walk.

Richard began, "Sonya, when did this restaurant seating thing start?"

Sonya looked up at him and said, "I really can't remember when it began. I have been bothered by it for as long as I can remember. Sometimes I get the perfect seat first off. Other times, it takes several moves before I feel comfortable and I get quite anxious, as you noticed tonight. Once I've found it, I'm fine."

"It's so interesting," added Richard. "What do you think causes it?"

"I really can't say. If I have the opportunity to scan the restaurant, I can usually determine within a matter of seconds where I'd prefer to sit – or more importantly – where I'd prefer *not* to sit," she offered. "You'll get a kick out of this. Sometimes, when the host gives me the option and asks me where I want to sit without having had the opportunity to scan the room beforehand, it feels as though my head does a full 360 degree rotation, like Linda Blair in *The Exorcist*. It's not a pretty picture and, in fact, I've been known to leave the restaurant when this happens. You know, it's just something that causes me angst. I can't explain it and the feeling goes away when I find a spot that is right. You know, perhaps it's that I can't let go… that I can't let go of my need to have a sense of control over the situation." She pondered this for a moment before looking at Richard again. "Whatever it is, thank you, Richard, for taking control tonight. You are a sweetheart."

Richard smiled back and began to think about what he may need to 'let go'.

Tom – *Running Into My 'Ex' Anxiety*

G reg caught up with Tom in Aisle 4 and asked, "You'll never guess who is in the next aisle."

Just by the tone of Greg's voice, Tom knew that it could be only one person: his ex-wife, Sheila. "Geez," he shouted under his breath. "I just can't seem to escape from her anywhere. What the heck is she doing in a build-it centre?" He could feel his blood begin to boil.

Although this was a rhetorical question, Greg did his best to answer. "Well, don't know, Tom. You could ask her. I think she's here with… uh… you know who."

"Oh great," Tom exclaimed. "She not only finds me in the only location in the entire city where I think I'm pretty sure she'll never set foot, she also has the nerve to show up with that loser she calls her boyfriend. What's his name again… Earl? Roy?"

"Ray," interrupted Greg. "Ray Doherty. You know who he is, Tom. He owns the fish and tackle place out on Front Street. You know… where we used to buy our fishing gear?"

Tom knew full well who Sheila was seeing these days. While he didn't know Ray personally, he knew him to be somewhat of a redneck despite the fact that he had the best-stocked fishing supply store in the vicinity.

Tom got back to task. He was looking for an electric timer for his sprinkler system and couldn't seem to find it. This was the last thing on his list and he didn't want to leave the store without it. However, he also did not want – under any circumstances – to bump into his ex-wife. But how on earth could he concentrate now that she was milling about?

His palms began to get cold and clammy and he could feel beads of sweat from underneath his baseball cap. The moment he realized he was having this reaction, his chest tightened and his stomach got tied up in knots which, of course, compounded the situation even more. Tom resented the fact that Sheila still had this effect on him. Still, after four-and-a-half years! he thought, beating up on himself. Why can't I let go? What does she still frustrate me so much?

Greg could tell that his friend was getting very tense and uncomfortable. "You OK, Tom?" he asked calmly. "We can go if you want."

"I'm not leaving until I get what I came for," he retorted. "Help me look for the timer."

"You got it, bud," Greg added as he began to search alongside Tom for the illusive timer.

Moments later, Greg found the timer in question. He handed it over to Tom to ensure that it was the right one.

"Nice," said Tom, relaxing a bit. "Where's Sheila now?" he asked as if Greg would know.

"No idea… I've been here with you," Tom replied.

"OK, let's get outta' here, then," he quietly barked at Greg over his shoulder as he made his way to the end of Aisle 4. Just as he was rounding the aisle corner toward the checkout counters, he noticed Sheila and Ray in line already at the only check-out that was open. Tom stopped in his tracks. A split-second later – not noticing that Tom had come to an abrupt stop – Greg came barrelling into him at full throttle, causing both of them to careen into the six-foot high display of antifreeze between them and the checkout. Aside from a few bottles dropping onto the floor, and Tom's basket of items flying into the air, they were left relatively unscathed. And, more importantly, they were not identified by Sheila or Ray.

"That was close," admitted Greg as they neared the checkout. They had picked up the displaced bottles of anti-freeze, put them back onto the display and retrieved Tom's items. By the time this was done, Sheila and Ray had left the store.

Tom was nearly back to normal, aside from a bit of mild anger and resentment that he held onto – directed at himself, not Sheila or Ray.

They left the store, and Tom smiled at Greg: "Thanks for the help."

"Any time," Greg smiled. "But what's this between you and Sheila? I thought things were over and done with and that you were OK with things."

"Yeah, I know," responded Tom. "Sometimes I still feel that I got shafted; that I'm still giving in somehow."

Greg hesitated yet added, "You gotta' let this go, man!"

"Don't worry, I'll be fine," Tom asserted. "I just need something else to focus on; my boat, the kids, the dogs… my fear only surfaces when I'm faced with actually running into her, confronting her. It's silly, but it is what it is. I'll get over it."

Tom and Greg hopped into Tom's jeep and headed toward their next stop.

Valerie – *Unexpected Vistor Anxiety*

Sunday afternoons were sacred to Valerie, and this one was no exception. She relished the idea of having the afternoon all to herself – to read, to meditate, to garden, to nap, to do anything she wanted. The only difficult thing was to decide what it was she wanted to spend her time doing.

The house needed cleaning, that was a certainty. The dinner party she and her husband, Cam, had hosted the evening before produced stacks of dirty dishes, glasses, stemware, serving platters, and cutlery, all needing attention. With the few breakfast and lunch dishes added to the pile, it was a sight that Valerie just didn't want to deal with today. And, of course, there were the bathrooms and just general cleaning that needed to be done.

It wasn't that Cam didn't help Valerie with the more mundane chores; he did. In fact, they shared most of the household tasks, including the dishes. Yet, today, Valerie was just not in the mood. The party was a success and a lot of work, so she wanted the day to relax. She wanted Cam to enjoy his Sunday afternoon golf game while she basked in her solitude. She didn't even have to worry about dinner; they had enough leftovers from the party to more than suffice.

It was a relatively cool afternoon, so she decided to pull out her book and curl up on the living room sofa with a nice cup of Chamomile tea. She was about two-thirds of the way through the book, and she was really enjoying it. She knew that she'd be able to finish it this afternoon. This pleased her because it would both allow her final closure on a book that seemed to take forever to finish, and provide her the opportunity to start the one she had to finish for her monthly book club, which was the week after next. I'd better get this one done today then, she thought to herself as she took the bookmark out and slid it into one of the back pages for safekeeping.

Valerie had just finished the first of her seven remaining chapters when she heard footsteps crossing the front porch toward the front door. She immediately sprang up from the sofa, dropping her book. Who can that be? she thought, alarmed. Oh God! The house is a mess!

In the time it took her to spring from the sofa and move halfway across the living room, she turned into a complete wreck. All she could think of was the mess. Mess everywhere. There were still a few dirty wine glasses, dessert plates, napkins and other party-fatigued items strewn around the room, and she didn't even want to think about the dining room, kitchen, family room... *chaos!*

She also thought about how anyone would have the gall to show up unannounced. She despised uninvited guests. Guests should call first! the voice inside her demanded. We always do, she insisted to herself. Cam and I wouldn't dream of just dropping in… on anyone. Family or friends!

As she approached the front door, she could feel her pulse racing and it was not a comfortable feeling. She also looked a mess. She hadn't applied any make-up and she had her long brown hair tossed back in a bright blue scrunchie. She was not an overly vain person, but she did like to be presentable, even to complete strangers. Why haven't they rung the doorbell yet? Can they see me? Maybe they went away, she thought frantically, as she tried to get a grip; it didn't seem to be working. Lucky that I at least put on my yoga gear and I'm not still in my nightie, she admitted to herself.

The doorbell finally rang. She was standing right behind the door trying to muster enough will to open it. She hesitated a moment – for two reasons. First, she didn't want whoever was out there to think that she was waiting for them. And secondly, pausing a little longer, she thought, I don't have to open it. I don't think they saw me. If I stay really quiet… The doorbell rang again.

"I know you're in there, Val," said a familiar voice from the other side of the door. "Open up!"

Valerie slid over to the sidelight and peered gently though the blind. Susan, she whispered, you know better!

Knowing who was at the door didn't help much. She prayed to God that Susan wasn't expecting to come in and visit. She liked Susan, it wasn't that. She just didn't like people showing up out of the blue.

As she opened the door, Valerie took a deep breath to try to slow herself down, including her inner self: her thoughts and emotions that were, for all intents and purposes, getting the best of her.

"Hey Val!" uttered Susan. "Sorry to drop by, but you know how it goes, I was in the neighbourhood, blah, blah…"

Valerie responded with a somewhat of an insincere smile and a very truncated, "No problem. What's up?"

Susan noticed that Valerie didn't appear too welcoming, and the light bulb went on. "Oh, Val, right!" She quickly started. "I'm so sorry. I – literally – was on my way to the market and I just wanted to drop off the book I borrowed from you. It was already in the car – I forgot to bring it in last night. I tried to call you on my cell before I arrived, but my battery must have died. Val, really, I'm sorry. I know you don't like people showing up uninvited."

"It's OK, Susan… it's ok," Valerie blurted, accepting Susan's sincere apologies. She remembered Susan mentioning the book last evening but didn't clue in that she might bring it over this afternoon.

She still felt anxious. She really didn't want Susan to stay. Valerie looked at Susan and met her outstretched hand, taking the book and uttering a sincere, "Thanks, Suze!"

With that, Susan gave Valerie a quick hug, turned and marched along the sidewalk towards her car. Valerie stood in the doorway as she watched her friend drive out of view. I wonder… what is it with me and this unexpected visitor thing? Why *do* I get so tense, so bothered, if someone just drops in? she reflected. After a few moments, it came to her. I just don't like to be caught unawares! I like to be prepared, not necessarily physically – the house, my clothes, my hair – but emotionally prepared to welcome people into my space, to be present for them. When people drop in unannounced, I'm simply not prepared.

She turned and walked back through the open door. She traced her steps back to the sofa, picked up her book and started the next chapter.

Maya and Drew – *D o g   A n x i e t y*

"hey are model parents, really. They shouldn't get so bent out of shape," Rex said to Daryl as their guests left for the evening. "They were only here for, what, a little more than three hours?"

"I know, but you know how they are," Daryl added. "They've both been like that ever since the girls arrived."

"You're right, but you'd think that after the first couple of years they'd ease up a bit," Rex offered. "I mean, they still hate leaving them at home, even for a few minutes. I think they are terribly overprotective."

"Well, who are we to judge, Rex?" admitted Daryl. "We don't have little ones to take care of who are totally dependent on us for every single thing in their lives."

"No, you've got a point," he agreed. "It's just that when we have them over, I'd like them to be able to totally and unconditionally enjoy themselves while they are here, and that doesn't seem to be the case, and I don't think it ever has been, or ever will be again."

Daryl said, "Oh, come on, Rex. Don't exaggerate. I think they enjoyed themselves tonight. They like our company, and we enjoy theirs. We always have stimulating conversation, fantastic food, drinks. They like coming over and spending time – don't worry about that, Rex."

"I guess you're right, but did you notice both of them constantly looking at their watches through dinner?" he asked.

"Yes, now that you mention it, that was kind of excessive, especially Drew. But again, we aren't proud parents, so we have no context," Daryl added.

Maya and Drew were the proud parents of two girls of the canine variety. The 'girls,' named Bella and Tika, were Golden Labs (2 and 3 years old, respectively), with beautiful coats, full, dark brown eyes; and temperaments that exuded amiability, energy and a *joie-de-vivre* that was utterly contagious. The women loved their little girls; they were a part of the family.

Spending time away from the girls was difficult for both Maya and Drew. Leaving them by themselves created such anxiety for Drew that Maya could not avoid falling into the trap herself. If Drew became anxious or nervous, Maya would pick up on it instantly and it would then become hers to deal with as well. It wasn't something they felt good about, but they dealt with it the best way they could because they loved their girls. Most times, they just didn't allow themselves to get into situations that would provoke or instigate the anxiety and guilt that they felt when separated from the pups. However, it wasn't always easy.

Dinner with Rex and Daryl was a bit of an exception. They had known the guys for fifteen years and were great friends. They had tried bringing the girls over one time, invited of course, which regrettably ended in disaster. Still pups, both Bella and Tika were so excited to see the guys that they left gift deposits of the liquid *and* solid sort on the brand new living room carpet. So that was no longer an option, and although they hosted the guys over at their place occasionally, they enjoyed Daryl's cooking and getting out of the house as well.

Maya and Drew had looked forward to this evening all week. Decked out in their designer jeans and tees, they bid the girls good-bye, giving each a big kiss and pat on the head. They both knew better than to look back, but as they did, they noticed both pairs of big brown eyes sullenly looking back at them, pleading for them not to leave them alone.

Maya, sensing that Drew was about to do or say something, interjected, "Let's get a move on. You know the guys don't appreciate tardiness," making a gentle dig at Rex's need for punctuality.

"OK, ok," quipped Drew, "I'm coming."

Seated around the massive kitchen island, Maya, Drew and Rex settled into yet another invigorating conversation. Daryl busied himself with the meal preparation, included in the group, but on the periphery of what was being discussed.

An hour into the evening, Drew looked at her watch. Sensing the trepidation setting in, Maya put a hand on Drew's arm for support. Daryl was still prepping for dinner and Drew was becoming anxious that it was going to be a really long evening. We really shouldn't have come, she thought. We can't leave the dogs for more than a couple of hours. Their poor little bladders will burst. Drew allowed the thoughts to race through her mind. Get a grip, Drew, she told herself. It's only been just over an hour.

Ten minutes later, the meal was served. For the first twenty minutes or so, Maya thought that Drew had settled down. All of a sudden, Drew looked at her watch again. Consciously or unconsciously, Drew, Maya, or both would glance down at their watches approximately every fifteen minutes from that moment on. Daryl and Rex became very aware of what was happening, but didn't let on. They both knew the girls well enough to know that it was no use arguing with them or presenting an alternate perspective. Instead, Daryl served dessert earlier than planned and they wrapped up dinner altogether shortly after ten o'clock.

Drew drove. They were home in less than fifteen minutes. They entered the house quietly and to their surprise, the pups were both sound asleep in their doggie beds. Drew thought to herself, Now, if we were certain this would happen every time...

Cara – *C o n f l i c t   A n x i e t y*

I t was happening again. She was in the middle of a situation that she could not seem to get herself out of. This always happens to me, Cara thought, extremely annoyed. Annoyed with herself and the situation. She should have seen it coming. Whenever her two cousins, Ruth and Theo, got together, there was trouble. As brothers and sisters go, Cara told herself, this pair takes the cake. They can't be in the same room together for more than two minutes without arguing.

Cara somehow thought that today would be different. It was her Aunt Ginnie's 80th Birthday. Ginnie was Ruth and Theo's mom, so one would think that they would at least try to get along with each other on this special occasion. Even if they hated each other, couldn't they just act civil toward each other for a couple of hours – for the sake of their own Mother? Cara quietly reflected, knowing full well that she should pipe up and say something to both of them directly. But that was not going to happen.

At the first inkling of conflict, Cara often feels a sort of tension in her chest and stomach. If the situation doesn't pass quickly, she becomes short of breath which, in turn, causes her to become disoriented, unfocused and extremely uncomfortable. When this happens, she feels a mild sense of panic and at times, she experiences the feeling as though she is caught in the 'fight or flight' dichotomy.

Cara had a definite opinion about what Ruth and Theo were arguing about but before she was put in the position to take sides, she found her exit route. She had just noticed someone exiting the restroom and she used that, and the empty cooler bottle she held in her hand, as a good excuse to claim her turn. She excused herself politely, overly exaggerating the word "b a t h r o o m" to the others so as not to disrupt the ongoing diatribe. Freedom! she thought to herself as she headed for the restroom.

Away from her quarrelling cousins at last, she breathed in deeply several times, calming herself. Her apprehension around conflict happened often enough that she could recognize the triggers and, consequently, put steps into action as soon as she could to remedy the situation. She was also smart enough to know that avoiding conflict was not the right path to take all of the time. In fact, she frequently felt frustrated and disappointed with herself for not standing up for what she believed in, for not being authentic and true to herself. It was even more than that sometimes. When it was just her and someone else and there was a disagreement or an argument, she became anxious when she felt that she may disappoint that person because of a decision she needed to make or an opinion she needed to share. Cara cared deeply for her friends and family: well, most of her family anyway. She really didn't care for Theo – she thought he was somewhat of a bully, and this opinion was often the jumping off point for many a conflict between the three of them. Yes, she cared deeply for the people who were around her; however, Cara also wanted to do what was best for her. She – like everyone else – was entitled to her opinion. Regardless, she rarely felt empowered enough to voice it.

Why can't everyone just get along? The world would be a much happier place, she rationalized. She quickly remembered someone responding to this statement by postulating: "Yes, but the world would be a much more boring place as well." I could live with 'boring,' Cara admitted to herself, smiling.

Coming out of the restroom a few minutes later – it was good that she went because, as it happens, she really did need to go – Cara looked towards where Ruth and Theo had been, and saw that they were no longer there. Ah, peace at last, she thought. Good. Aunt Ginnie wouldn't have to be a witness to their ongoing battles.

The birthday party ended on a very positive note, without any other major disruptions. Unbelievably, Theo had an issue with the kind of cake Ruth had purchased, but before that could escalate into full-blown fisticuffs, Aunt Ginnie blew out the candles – all eighty of them – thereby diffusing the rant in the cheers and hoorays of the guests who surrounded her.

On her way home Cara drove by the community college. She hadn't noticed the new advertisement until just then, which read: "Conflict Resolution for Work and Home, Classes Begin Soon, Enrol Today." Now, I never thought of that, she admitted to herself. I wonder if a class would really help.

"What the heck! I'm going to give it a go," she exclaimed to herself as she drove by. "What do I have to lose?" Cara instantly felt relieved. She instinctively knew that this was going to be her first step in dealing with her conflict anxiety.

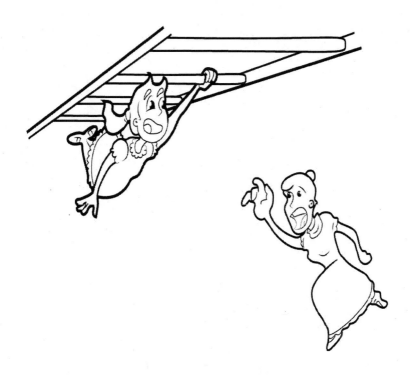

Heather – *O v e r p r o t e c t i v e   M o m   A n x i e t y*

She was unconsciously holding her breath watching intently as her 7-year old daughter, Sam, dangled precariously from the monkey bars. She was at the school playground, along with several other neighbourhood parents and their kids, enjoying the first sunny day in what seemed like months. The large playground was part of a bigger city park that was located adjacent to Sam's elementary school, a short ten minute walk from their house.

Sam's Mom, Heather, couldn't understand why she insisted on playing on this 'contraption.' She thought it was an accident just waiting to happen; the sharp edges, the height. It must be a full seven feet off the ground, she thought to herself. She knew that one day something horrible would occur – that Sam would fall and split her head open or break her collar bone or lose a tooth. Her mind drifted off thinking about all of the unpleasant things that *could* happen to her little girl when Sam leapt down off of the monkey bars and scrambled toward the slide, jarring Heather back to the present.

Heather admitted to herself that the playground was a godsend to her and her husband, Geoff, and the dozens of other families that took advantage of the sprawling park. The park contained a baseball diamond, a soccer field, picnic areas, a wading pool, swings, the jungle gym contraption, and other *safer* play equipment. Nevertheless, she would feel better if a few of Sam's friends would come over to play in their back yard, despite the fact that the only fun thing it offered to the rambunctious neighbourhood children was an old tire swing that hung from an outstretched branch of the towering oak tree that was anchored in the centre of their small backyard. Yes, but that is such a fun swing! Heather thought to herself as she looked over to see Sam race with a few of the other kids toward the children's swing set.

Cheryl, Heather's neighbour and friend, noticing that Heather was quiet and withdrawn, sauntered toward her and gave her a nudge with her elbow. "What are you so quiet about?"

Heather looked at her friend and admitted, "Oh, I just get the willies when Sam uses that stupid jungle gym over there. It's just a train wreck waiting to happen, you know?"

Cheryl smiled. She knew where this was coming from. Sam was an only child and Heather was scared shirtless that some terrible harm would come to her daughter. They'd had that conversation before and Cheryl knew to tread carefully. Heather admitted to being overprotective, and felt embarrassed and silly at hearing herself admit it out loud.

"Oh, it's safe, you know. The City wouldn't have installed it otherwise" offered Cheryl matter-of-factly. "Cindy and Bobby are always on it and they've never come home with so much as a scratch."

"I know, but they're older," Heather replied. "It's the height... what if she falls? She could really do some serious damage!"

"Well, kids will be kids, Heather" Cheryl quipped as she looked over to the swing set where her son was stationed with Sam. She cited the popular maxim hoping that it would calm Heather's nerves just a wee bit. Cheryl noticed Heather draw a deep breath as she, too, looked over to where her daughter was now playing.

Cheryl knew Heather and Geoff pretty well; they'd been neighbours for about five years now. For all intents and purposes, Heather *was* overprotective of Sam. This wasn't so much of a judgment than a concerned observation. Heather got so nervous and anxious about Sam's every movement all of the time, and she had been that way for Sam's entire life. Ever since she was born, Heather would always have Sam in her sightline, always. I wonder if that's what having only one child must feel like, Cheryl reflected.

Half an hour later, Heather and Sam said 'good-bye' to Cheryl, Cindy and Bobby, and struck out on their short walk home. Sam, in her usual manner, hopped and skipped around Heather as they made their way home. Somewhere behind Heather, Sam asked her Mom if she could have a snack as soon as they got back. Before she could answer, Heather heard a 'thump' and then a loud wail coming from her little girl's lungs. Sam had tripped on a piece of sidewalk, fell on her bare hands, and scraped her left knee. Heather's heart went into high gear and she instantly felt a huge pressure weigh on her, centred in her stomach. She jumped into action and tried to calm Sam down, almost screaming herself. She grabbed her in her arms while taking an inventory of her injuries. She quickly ascertained that the two cuts on her wrists and the one on her knee were all surface scrapes.

"You have to be more careful Sam!" she blurted out in a voice that was much louder and abrasive than she intended.

She pulled out a clean tissue from her pocket and carefully dabbed blood and dirt away from the cuts, which seemed to ease Sam's fear.

"Feel better?" she said giving her daughter a quick hug.

"Yup, but can I still have a snack?" she questioned, as if this incident would have caused her mother to second guess the request.

Heather smiled affirmatively at Sam and began to take deep breaths, which tempered the rapid beating of her heart. The pressure in her stomach subsided as they neared home but the embarrassment of how she had reacted to this insignificant incident continued to niggle at her. Will I always be so paranoid? she reflected momentarily. She smiled to herself and thought: well, perhaps only for another ten or twelve years.

Cliff – *Forgetting to do Something I Said I Would Anxiety*

Seated on the bench that overlooked the wide, expansive valley nestled several hundred feet below him and the rolling hills off in the distance, Cliff admitted to himself that he deserved this break. He enjoyed hiking and this particular trek offered him the solitude and reflection time he rarely had the opportunity to capture for himself.

It was a beautiful summer day, not too hot, with blue skies dotted with puffy white clouds. It was going on eleven o'clock in the morning and it was a perfect time for a quick 'sustenance' break before he started on the second leg of his three-leg hike. He enjoyed hiking the wilderness trails that twisted and meandered for several kilometres on the outskirts of town, especially because they were still new to him and thus offered him a challenging trek, great exercise and the opportunity for time alone. Of course, he hiked safely, being sure to bring the right survival gear, food and H$_2$O with him in his lightweight rucksack.

Chomping down on the last bit of his nutrition bar, Cliff crumpled the wrapper and put it in his pack for recycling. He took a swig of water from his canister, closed his eyes and settled into his momentary meditation of sorts. His mind wandered and as it did so, he tried to close off his thoughts to any- and everything.

This euphoric feeling of peacefulness – although sublime – was short-lived. A split second later, Cliff bolted upright off the bench, nearly flinging himself over the edge of the promontory and onto the ledge of rock and boulders perched a good hundred feet below.

"#@&%!" he barked out loud, not thinking or caring if any person, plant or animal was in earshot of his profanity. "I can't believe I did it again! I am an idiot! Damn it... when will I ever learn?"

If it were that he just got temporarily angry with himself, that would be one thing. But it didn't stop there. Cliff's anger at himself, which was, indeed, bad enough, quickly morphed into a deep, unfathomable personal dislike of himself as a person, and his abilities as a professional. This deep-seated self-loathing caused Cliff such angst that his body began to shake and, for a few moments, he thought he was going to pass out due to a lack of oxygen.

He was momentarily paralysed. He couldn't move. He couldn't control, or even regain, his thoughts. His eyes were open but he couldn't see a thing. An immense wave of overwhelmedness blanketed him as if another hiker found him on the trail and covered him with a very heavy, lead-filled mantle. However, this blanket was not soothing, nor comfortable. This blanket was heavy and oppressive. It made it even more difficult for him to breathe.

Slowly, Cliff began to think about his breathing. In fact, he realized that he was barely breathing at all. He proceeded to take long, deep breaths; counting to ten, inhaling, holding for a second or two, and then counting to ten, exhaling, and so on.

The ebb and flow of this conscious breathing exercise seemed to work. He began to feel himself again… that is, until his thoughts travelled back to the instance when this all began. He tried to trace his thoughts back to what it was that jolted him out of his peaceful reverie.

Cliff had committed to completing an evaluation review for one of his major clients, due the day before. Cliff promised 'add-ons' like this all of the time. He thought of them as value added service: service that set him apart from his competitors. The fact that it was an add-on, a 'freebie', didn't matter to Cliff. In fact, his client was rather non-committal herself about the review but, again, that was of no consequence. If Cliff Hollister said he will do something, by gosh, Cliff Hollister does it, he whispered to himself while packing up.

The internal conversation that Cliff was having with himself – some would call it negative self talk – lasted until he walked through the door of his 7th floor condominium, approximately 45 minutes later. In a real funk, he sauntered into his office and looked through the pile of papers and files that had accumulated on top of his desk. Weeding through the short stack, he noticed a neon pink Post-it Note™ out of the corner of his eye, pulled it out and read the short message: "Review for Alisyn – FRIDAY".

"So," he reassured himself out loud a bit too late, "I *did* write it down." Since the forgetting-to-follow-up-and-therefore-not-live-up-to-his-word issue had happened a few times before, with embarrassing and costly results, Cliff had devised a simple method to ensure that he would not find himself in the same mess again: he got into the habit of writing important messages down on neon pink Post-it Notes™. A hideous colour, he admitted to himself, but the process was simple and had worked, up until now.

Cliff realized quickly that it was his failure to arrange the stack of papers that proved to be the real culprit. He planned on calling Alisyn on Monday to apologize, knowing full well that she may have even forgotten about his commitment. Even so, his self perception of his integrity was at stake, so he had to make amends even if just for his own sense of well being.

Cliff completed the review and forwarded it via email to his client. After that, he called a few of his friends and arranged a poker night. Life's too short, he finally admitted to himself, hoping that if something like this happened again, he'd be aware enough not to let it take him so deeply so quickly.

Jake – *U n e x p e c t e d   C h a n g e   A n x i e t y*

After parking his car, Jake strolled across the street toward the medical building that housed his doctor's office. He didn't like getting his physical but knew that it was better to go through the motions than listen to his partner go on and on about it if he didn't succumb. Besides, he was smart enough to know that it was a good thing to be in the habit of doing every couple of years.

He entered the lobby of the 16-story building and headed to the bank of elevators. He got in and rode the elevator to the 11th floor, held the door open on the 8th floor for an elderly couple, and continued on his journey skyward. Landing on eleven, he crossed the elevator threshold and made his way down the hall. Once inside the sunny but small reception room, he sauntered up to the desk, left his name with one of the three clerks on duty and took a seat in a chair that offered breath-taking views of the city.

Jake looked up from the two-year old 'Scientific American' magazine he was thumbing through, thinking to himself, It's bad enough that they don't invest in good mags, but at least get something that's current. He then remembered reading somewhere that the germs that resided on magazines and books in doctor's offices were a major culprit of the cross contamination of human viruses, such as the flu. Jake smirked to himself, quickly discarded the magazine, and reached for the hand sanitizer dispenser.

He was listening to the piped in music while he waited for the clerk to come out and retrieve him. The clock on the wall behind receptionist area read 10:22. Late, but not unusually late, he thought to himself, knowing that a wait at the doctor's office is par for the course.

A few moments later, as he was about to look at the clock again, he noticed a bit of a commotion in the reception area. The clerk who had taken his name, now 31 minutes earlier, beckoned him to the counter. As he approached, Jake's stomach began to turn, a feeling of nausea beginning to emanate through his entire being.

"Mr. Compton?" asked the clerk, curtly.

"Yes, I'm Jake Compton" affirmed Jake, making no eye contact.

"Dr. Cheung has had to leave. We'll have to reschedule your appointment." asserted the clerk, nonchalantly.

Jake's head started to pound. He responded, his voice shaking, "But I'm here, right now! I can't wait. Can't he wait 'til we're done? It shouldn't take long. I've driven all this way…"

He stopped there as he soon realized that he had driven a total of two kilometres to get to the appointment. He began to feel overly emotional for some reason.

"I'm very sorry, Mr. Compton. You see, Dr. Cheung has to respond to an emergency at the hospital. The emergency is, as you can understand, more urgent than your physical this morning."

Jake knew she was right. I must seem like an idiot, he thought to himself. But this is so frustrating. Why can't things ever work out according to the plan.

He looked at the clerk and implored, "Can another doctor do the physical?"

"Unfortunately, that's not possible." she responded in a kind yet insistent tone. She continued, "Jake, the other doctors each have their own full patient load today, and besides, you are Dr. Cheung's patient; he would like to see you himself, I would guess."

"Ya, right… I guess." Jake agreed hesitantly. He just couldn't see the point of going to the effort of making appointments, putting them in a schedule, arriving on time, etc., if they were going to be cancelled. I mean, what's the point? he pondered as he tapped his fingers on the counter clearly revealing his growing agitation at the unexpected change in events.

Jake really did dislike unexpected change. He liked his life pretty much planned out. That's not to say that he was inflexible, but he detested last minute modifications or variations. If things had to change, at least give him some upfront warning. According to Jake, it was just common courtesy.

He made another appointment with the clerk for a date and time just a few days away, which seemed to settle him a bit. He took the appointment slip from the clerk's outstretched hand, said "Thanks", and made a B-line for the office door.

The nausea seemed to have calmed down a bit but his head was still throbbing. He felt embarrassed for reacting the way he did, and immature. He also felt a bit as though he couldn't control himself, especially when his head started to pound.

Jake was making his way back to his car when he thought of something that his mother had once told him, "Jake," he remembered her saying, "we only have control over how we react to any given situation." He reflected: this makes so much sense now. Would these words of wisdom work next time? he asked himself. Perhaps, if I remember them in time, he noted.

He started his car and rolled down all four windows to allow the cool spring air to circulate throughout the car. Filling his lungs with fresh air as he drove, he thought about his mother's wise words again and realized that he has a bit of work to do with respect to transforming his reaction to unexpected changes. I'd like to get to the place where I don't react like a 'mad man,' he admitted to himself, considering that a goal he could live with.

Grace – 'TP' *Anxiety*

Grace DaSilva is, according to her colleagues, friends and acquaintances, "well put together". She is a partner in a successful law firm that is located in one of the most glamorous office towers in the city. She lives in a beautiful two-bedroom condominium which offers her a commanding panoramic view of the city and ocean. She eats out in the finest establishments and can afford high quality couture, and shoes. Her friends fondly describe her as the Carry Bradshaw of Vancouver, a comparison she is happy and proud to live up to.

Grace is 31 years old, captivating and currently, unattached. She possesses an Ava Gardner 'natural' beauty that, while complimented by make-up, requires little, if any. She stands five feet, ten inches tall – *sans stilettos* – has a gorgeous figure, and turns heads (of both genders) when she enters a room, be that a boardroom, a restaurant or the tennis club. And to top it all off, she is an incredibly kind and well respected humanitarian and volunteer.

You would think that there would be some people who would despise Grace; be envious, even jealous of her looks and her accomplishments. But everyone who knows, or comes in contact with Grace, would argue the contrary. Some would say that Grace is... well... *perfect*.

Not Grace. Everyone has their own skeleton buried deep in their closet. No one is perfect in this world, according to Grace, especially her. No, not even close. Grace is very aware of her hidden skeleton... this thing she calls her 'TP Trepidation' – her absolute anxiety of being without toilet paper – not if, but when – duty calls.

This dread, this complete and body paralyzing angst began manifesting itself when Grace was in high school. She was an accomplished athlete, did well academically, and dated boys from the 'in crowd'. Grace was popular, and with this popularity came notoriety, which in and of itself was not a bad thing, but when her anxiety began to surface, it also became something that she was known for.

Personal hygiene was of immense importance to Grace, probably ingrained in her as a small child. Knowing this, a few of her tenth grade classmates from gym class decided to play a practical joke on her and would, on several occasions, hide the toilet paper from the cubicles in the girl's washroom leaving Grace to often fend for herself. This meant that she either 1) had to go without or 2) trip over to the paper towel dispenser and use the paper's abrasive surface instead. Regardless of the choice, Grace would leave the washroom in tears, humiliated and broken.

You see, the thing wasn't necessarily that it happened because she knew that it would. The concern was that she never knew *when* it was going to happen again. She was in constant fear of not having access to proper toilet paper. And she wasn't always in a situation where she could carry it with her, especially at school.

The TP 'skeleton' remained with her until she left high school. It didn't scar her for life, it just made things much more difficult for a teenager to deal with during those impressionable years.

Now, fast-forward to Grace in adult life. One could wonder why she still considers her 'TP Trepidation' a continuing skeleton. Only a couple of her closest friends know of Grace's ongoing angst and would never play such a horrible prank on her like those she experienced in high school. They, too, know how Grace reacts when toilet paper has gone innocently missing from restaurant lavatories, tennis club change rooms, etc.: she loses all composure; she starts to feel short of breath, and with this comes light-headedness. Worse yet, she starts to cry incessantly, causing quite a commotion for others in close proximity. These reactions, in turn, cause extreme embarrassment which takes her hours to get over.

Luckily, Grace has managed to come up with a solution that works well for her. She has got into the habit of buying bigger handbags; handbags that can easily conceal a small packet of tissues that, when called upon, can easily and comfortably take the place of absent toilet paper. It also helps that Grace seldom finds herself frequenting locations where there may be a lack of toilet paper on hand. However, on occasion, when she does, she is confident that regardless if the bathroom is fully stocked or not, she came fully prepared to use the restroom with complete confidence that her 'TP Trepidation' will not rear its ugly head.

No one is perfect, not even Grace DaSilva.

Mansour – *R e t i r e m e n t   A n x i e t y*

Leaning against the door to his boss' office, Mansour – "Manny" – Dawali waited anxiously for his director, TJ, to finish the call he was on. TJ motioned for Manny to wait. With his index finger pointing upward, TJ mouthed the word "one minute", so Manny knew that the call should only take another minute or so. He was used to his boss' sign language; over the years, they had gotten into a communication pattern that was both effective and comfortable at the same time.

Manny was uneasy. He had come to TJ's office this morning to let TJ know that he had decided to retire from his post as facilities manager of the Green Valley School Board, effective in four months' time. TJ had had 'the conversation' with Manny four years ago, when he hit his 'thirty years of service' milestone, but Manny doubted very much that TJ expected he would retire quite so soon. He was only 53 years old, and in four months, he would reach thirty-five years of service. Thirty-five years is a long time, he reasoned.

This was not an easy decision for Manny. He had been at the board for almost thirty-five years and he loved his job: the people he worked with; his boss, TJ, was very good to him; the kids… They were good kids, he thought to himself, quietly reflecting on how respectful he thought the children were, at least the kids in his schools.

Although he'd gone over it a thousand times in his head, Manny suddenly began to feel as though he was making the wrong decision. He looked at TJ and felt as though he was betraying him, his team, the organization. He began to fidget with the loose change in his pocket. He stepped away from the doorframe and paced back and forth in the short hallway in front of TJ's office, all the while making a louder, more pronounced, jingling noise with his coins.

Manny, having retreated into his own little world, didn't even hear or notice TJ click his mobile phone closed and place it back into his hip holster. A moment passed, and then TJ cleared his throat with a quick "hum, hugm," which served to pull Manny back to the here and now.

"You OK, Manny?" asked TJ with a slight smile.

"Ya, boss… just got something to talk to you about, if now is a good time," Manny said, a bit dazed as if coming out of a deep dream.

"Sure, close the door and pull up a chair. You know the drill, no formalities in this office," he stated, leaning over to put his laptop into 'sleep' mode.

Yep, thought Manny to himself, how many guys have bosses who turn their computer off when you come in to talk? He was even more convinced that he was making a mistake. But he was here. He had to go through with it... it was the right thing to do, he assured himself as he took a seat.

Exactly seventeen minutes later, Manny opened the door to TJ's office and began the short trek back to his office on the floor above. Well, that didn't hurt, he thought as he reached for the stairwell door.

His department was a busy one, especially with the state of the school buildings in his community, so Manny didn't have much idle time to sit and think about his decision: a decision that was now final. As soon as he started up the engine to his new Ford F150 at the end of his busy day, and drove out of the parking lot toward home, he began to tense up. A few moments later, his hands felt cold and clammy. He thought back to the meeting with his boss. . .

TJ was disappointed, but understood. He had made a few jokes about Manny's young age, which Manny took in good stride. Overall, TJ was very supportive. He even went so far as to make an appointment with human resources, on Manny's behalf, to ensure that his exiting strategy was going to be a smooth one, especially when it came to pensions and health benefits. At the end of the meeting, TJ stood up, extended his hand, and wished Manny all the best in his retirement. Manny could not have wanted, nor expected, a better outcome in his meeting with TJ.

On his way home, he decided to take a short detour for a few moments and park his truck at a scenic lookout that was situated on the side of the main road that took him from the office to his home, about 22 kilometres away. He turned off the engine, and sat staring out over the view of the rolling hills and river that bordered the road as it wound its way into the city. Why do I feel so apprehensive, so anxious? he pondered. Manny quickly came to the realization that he was worried about what retirement would do to him. He had heard stories of people who, days after retirement, dropped dead, and he did not want to be one of them. He wondered what he would do with himself. He questioned whether the department would run as efficiently as it did right now, knowing full well that he only played one part in its success. He wondered if he would be bored out of his skull without the routine of going to work every day. He was concerned that his brain would go to mush and that he would shrivel up into a wrinkled old prune.

He laughed out loud, quickly putting a stop to the crazy thoughts that were tormenting him, filling his mind with useless, stupid scenarios that were so far-fetched and completely absurd. I didn't think I could be so melodramatic, he thought momentarily with a grin.

And then he thought about his wife and his kids (he had three grown children, with five beautiful grandchildren) and the possibilities. He enjoyed golf and tennis and fishing, and even more so, he enjoyed travelling with his wife.

Enough of mindless negative stuff Manny! he said to himself in a scolding manner as he started the engine. Retirement is what I want to make it, he reflected as he turned back onto the highway, feeling more at-ease and together. It's more of an attitude than anything else, he realized. Then and there, Manny chose to change the stigma of age-old retirement complacency into an outlook of retirement opportunity and renewal.

Tanika – *M a s s   S w i m   S t a r t   A n x i e t y*

She gave her wetsuit one last tug as she pulled it over her tall, lanky frame. Her body was suited for swimming, and she knew it. People referred to Tanika as 'the human dolphin': sleek, skilled and purposeful. She was fast in the water, and she revelled in swimming as a competitive sport. Admittedly, she did have a competitive streak and, according to those who knew her, thought of it as a waste of time if you were not in a competition to win. She was forty-three years old, and she'd been a competitor since high school.

It was Thursday morning, six o'clock to be exact, and Tanika had just arrived at the local beach with a few of her friends. The five of them were there to get in one last swim practice before the Seattle Triathlon, which was taking place in just two days' time. The five of them had been taking part in the triathlon every year religiously for the past twelve years, and they were all looking forward to the competition, the adrenaline rush, and exceeding their personal bests.

Of the three sports, Tanika was best at swimming. However, she ran and cycled extremely well, usually reaching the finish line well before a couple of her friends. When it came to swimming, she rarely finished last whether in a race with her friends, or in a competition with the other triathletes who took part in the Seattle event. In fact, when it came to the swim portion of the Seattle Triathlon, she usually came in first, or a very close second.

Tanika is a confident swimmer; that is for certain. But there is something that always seems to get under her skin just before the swimming leg of any triathlon. Before the start whistle blows, Tanika always worries whether she has positioned herself correctly so that she does not get swam over by any of the other competitors. With swimming, as with most competitive courses, the closer the position is to the inside of the course (or track, etc.) the faster the swimmers are, and the shorter the course ends up being.

For her, this fear of getting swum over while in the midst of competition is unbelievably nerve-wracking. She often gets to the point where she asks herself, What the heck am I doing here? Why am I doing this to myself? When this happens, inevitably, Tanika has to pee – again and again and again – which is not so easy to do in a full wetsuit. This need to relieve herself at the very last moment intensifies as a result of her having to pace back and forth continuously before the race begins. She has a hard time staying in one place for very long in anticipation of the mass swim start.

The thought of ramming into someone mid-swim is also very scary. Tanika has been elbowed a couple of times, which always takes her off guard and causes her to lose concentration, which in turn causes her to lose speed and confidence, which then shows in the final results – her ending up far from first or second place when the anxiety gets the best of her. In practice, it's not so bad, but in competition, it may signify losing the entire triathlon altogether.

This morning, she is practicing with, and against, her four friends, three of whom are stiff contenders. Trish, the fourth, excels at cycling, followed by running, and then swimming. Tanika always gives Trish a hard time and jokes about her porpoise-like swimming technique. Trish just takes it in stride because she usually beats Tanika in either running or cycling, and when she is at her best, both.

In an effort to ease her mass swim start anxiety, Tanika has recently begun to get into the habit of getting to the beach or course (if it is a competition) early so that she can take a few quiet moments to scan the entire course. This enables her to visualize where she is going to position herself at the start of the race. After visualizing her starting position, she 'gets in her head,' and envisions the race: the course, her swim, the other competitors. She allows herself to envision the swim going extremely well, without the fear of the possibility of someone swimming over her or elbowing her entering her thoughts.

Tanika performed this exercise prior to the three practice races she and her friends swam this morning. And although much easier with just four others swimming alongside her, Tanika thought that all three of the races went extremely well. In fact, by the time the third race was over, she was a full four lengths in front of her closest opponent. So far, so good, she thought to herself as she strode out of the water, grasping for the towel that Trish was offering her.

The Seattle Triathlon was hard and gruelling. Trish did well in both running and cycling, coming in at eleventh and ninth, respectively. Swimming, on the other hand, turned out to be a 'joke', she thought afterwards, placing a forty-nine out of 195 entrants.

Tanika performed really well in both running and cycling. In swimming, she managed a second place, and she was ecstatic. She reflected on the day, and how she prepared for the competition. In her mind, she systematically went through her scanning routine and spent a few moments returning to her visualizations. Could I have done something different? she thought to herself, forever the consummate competitor. In the end, she realized that she achieved her personal best. She did not encounter a single 'swim over,' and she ended up with a sixth place overall.

Not bad for forty-three! she admitted proudly to herself as she looked at the score sheet arm in arm with her four friends at her side.

Mark – *Public Speaking Anxiety*

The audience clapped appreciatively as Mark left the podium and started to make his way back to his seat. Once at his table, his boss, Susan, stood up and extended her hand and Mark shook it tentatively. She leaned over and said quietly in his ear, "That wasn't so bad, now was it?" Mark turned to her and smiled. It actually hadn't gone that badly, Mark thought to himself.

There was a ten minute break before the next speaker was scheduled to take the podium and Susan took this opportunity to acknowledge Marks's efforts. She waited while Mark took another mouthful of coffee to get his attention and told him that his presentation on their organization's sustainability initiative was "really, very good." She added that it was to the point, yet interesting and well-delivered. She mentioned that she especially liked the way he handled the tough questions posed by one of the VPs in attendance.

Susan knew that Mark had had a rough time of it when it came to public speaking; however, today, she was sincerely impressed and she wanted him to know it. Mark took a deep breath and settled back into his chair. He appreciated Susan's recognition and gave her a quick smile and a "Thank You."

While he led the sustainability and environmental programs for the organization and really knew his stuff, Mark still felt very uncomfortable relaying what he knew to others in a public forum, be it colleagues or complete strangers. What Susan had failed to notice, or probably more to the point, mention, when she shook his hand was that Mark's palm was wet with sweat. Had he not been wearing his suit jacket, she, and most of the other 175 people in attendance, would have definitely noticed the dark perspiration stains under each of his armpits. But he thought to himself, No, it wasn't so bad. I didn't vomit this time, my heart rate was elevated but not tachycardic, and I stayed pretty cool throughout the presentation even when asked those two unrelated questions by Bill Martin, the VP.

Later that day, when he had a few moments to himself, Mark reflected on the day and on his public speaking anxiety, specifically remembering when the sense of sheer doom at being asked to speak in front of a group actually began. It only took a split second. It was fifth grade. He knew it for a fact. He could remember clearly the first time he was ever asked to present in front of a group. The group was his fellow fifth graders and the presentation was a book report.

Perhaps, at the time, it was a lack of self-confidence; perhaps it was the fear of being laughed at; perhaps he was shy back then; or perhaps he wasn't prepared. Regardless, the mere thought of speaking in front of others caused him to blush, feel nauseous, and, in fact, actually vomit on more than one occasion. From time to time, his hands would tremble, so much so that his notes would flail out of control, becoming distracting both for him and the people in his audience. At times, his heart rate would increase so much so that he could barely focus. After his talks, presentations or speeches, even to this day, he felt silly and insecure, sometimes getting upset at himself for feeling this way.

The good news is that while Mark may not be completely comfortable, he is learning to reduce the anxiety associated with his public speaking. On a suggestion from a friend's meditation guide, he practiced deep breathing before a presentation he led about two years ago, and it seemed to help. It brought his heart rate down and allowed him to stay focused and actually have some fun. Along with deep breathing, which has become a regular practice, he also engages in positive self talk and visualization — not the kind where a nude audience is envisaged. He visualizes an engaged and content audience, one that appreciates and applauds his efforts. Much like what happened today, he thought, pleased with himself.

Kathryn – *Workload Anxiety*

Walking back from lunch, Kathryn thought to herself how much she enjoyed her lunch dates with the office crowd: Anne, Kim, Steve and Tamara. She loved getting together at the local bistro with her colleagues, who, in the past couple of years, had become friends, to see what was new on the menu, share some great food, and more importantly, engage in some lively conversation. Starting with 'shop talk,' the conversation had continued with family talk and ended a short forty-eight minutes later with a group declaration that they "should do this more often." They walked the two blocks back to the office in a group huddle, nearly tripping over each others' toes, laughing while still trying to maintain the semblance of a conversation.

Yes, Kathryn enjoyed these outings. She always came back to the office feeling refreshed and energized. In recent months, however, these excursions were becoming few and far between: too much to do and not enough of her to go around.

As she entered her office, Kathryn noticed that the red voice mail light on her telephone was blinking at her. She made a growling noise under her breath and had a sneaking suspicion that there was more than one message that begged for her attention. She lifted the receiver, punched in her security code and, *voila*, she was right. Three messages! She'd get to them later. She was surprised, in fact, that no one had called her on her mobile. Wait, she thought, as she reached for her cell phone, which had now dropped to the lower recesses of her huge, but very fashionable, purse. She pushed the 'on' button and a moment later saw that she had three voice, several text, and some email messages. Darn technology, she thought to herself as she began to feel increasingly overwhelmed. And I haven't even looked at my computer yet, she thought. The lightness that she had felt during lunch had all but disappeared in less than two short minutes.

She tapped her keyboard and her computer screen awoke from its lunchtime siesta. Instantly, she saw that there were eleven new emails waiting for her in her inbox. Eleven! How can that be? she thought to herself as she slumped in her chair; I've only been gone an hour. These new interruptions, in addition to the three meetings she was to attend this afternoon, plus the report that was due by the end of the week, not to mention the software training she had to participate in, and the fact that her assistant, Todd, was still on a steep learning curve, made for a very frustrating outlook on her immediate future. She knew she had to get a grip on things, but how? The sense of overwhelmedness and frustration muddied her thinking. Everywhere she looked she was reminded of the extent of her burgeoning workload.

Kathryn knew that she was not the only one dealing with some sort of workload-related anxiety. Everyone was busy. Everyone worked long hours and, for the most part, no one really complained. Knowing this was a consolation. Realizing that everyone was virtually in the same boat seemed to ease her frustration. And there were moments of fun – like today at lunch – and periods when the workload didn't seem as intense. But that wasn't today, or even this month, for that matter.

Not wanting to startle her, Todd lightly knocked on Kathryn's door, interrupting her quiet reflection. "I'm heading out for lunch," he said. "I just wanted to remind you of your 1:30 meeting with Finance."

Kathryn looked up, registered his presence, and said "Thank you, Todd. I'll be there." She looked at her watch. She had twenty minutes before she had to leave for the meeting. Instead of groaning and living into the frustration, Kathryn surprised herself by quickly playing her voice messages and reviewing both the text and email notes that had come in. Nothing urgent. She made a short list of messages she had to return and prioritized what she felt she could accomplish in the time that remained of her afternoon. She felt good at this small step.

On the way to the meeting, Kathryn thought about the times when she experienced this anxiety, this frustration about work. For the most part, it was centred around her perceived lack of control over things. Interesting, she murmured to herself. It was interesting that the word 'perceived' came into her consciousness. But it was true. When she felt she didn't have any control, she would start to feel overwhelmed and discouraged. However, when she took control – even over the simplest of things like prioritizing her 'to do' list for the afternoon – she felt a sense of autonomy and freedom. It really was about keeping everything in perspective. She worked hard, met her deadlines (well… most of them), and was a valued employee.

Kathryn entered the meeting room and noticed that Steve sat in a chair on the opposite side of the room. She made her way around the table and sat down in the empty seat beside him. She elbowed him lightly and said, "It was great getting out for lunch. I don't know about you, but it helps me put things in perspective. We really should do it more often."

Roger – *Being Late Anxiety*

The clock mounted on his office wall indicated 10:15 am. He checked his own wristwatch just to be doubly sure. It was common knowledge that the clocks in the office complex had minds of their own. His watch substantiated 10:15; he could trust his watch: it was expensive and Swiss. The muscles located just under his left eye started twitching with mild agitation. This was a sign.

Diane was supposed to drop by Roger's office at 10:15 am on-the-nose to pick him up. That would give them exactly forty-five minutes to get to their appointment with the corporate lawyer, whose office was located on the opposite side of town. The traffic, coupled with finding a parking spot mid-morning, was stressful at the best of times, let alone under a time constraint. Typically the jaunt only took around 35-40 minutes door to door, but you can never be too sure. And, of course, Diane insisted on driving again. Which was probably a good thing, as Roger's two-seater was piled high with items that still needed to be taken to the nearest Goodwill.

Roger didn't have a particularly sound sleep the night before. The neighbour's dog, an undistinguishable male cross of four different breeds, woke him out of his slumber at 3:14 am, exactly. He tossed and turned after that until the FM channel of his alarm clock startled him with the blaring sound of the morning news at 6:30. He hit the snooze button and opted to stay in bed for some additional shuteye, which he realized, as soon as he dragged himself from bed, was a mistake. He not only didn't get back to sleep, he missed his morning workout, to boot! He always felt like a million bucks after his workout and knew that exercise, sleep, and eating right were necessary to keep stress and anxiety at bay. He should have known better. But, he thought to himself, there's nothing I can do about it now.

He glanced down at his watch again. Four minutes had passed. It was now 10:19. We are cutting it too close, Roger said to himself. If we don't leave pretty darned soon – like in the next minute or two – we will not get there on time.

Roger was *always* on time. He prided himself on his punctuality. He, quite simply, did not like to keep people waiting. Oh, there was the odd time when he arrived exactly on time, but that was not the norm. He usually arrived at any appointment – chiropractic, dentist, dinner with friends, his weekly tennis match, it didn't matter what the occasion was – at least 10 minutes prior to the confirmed meeting time. And he expected others should show the same respect and often got quite miffed if others made him wait or, worse yet, stood him up altogether. He was working on this self-professed weakness, and was actually getting better at forgiving people for random acts of (slight) tardiness. Emergencies do come up. But if the emergency weren't life or death, then it took Roger longer to absolve people of this specific idiosyncrasy. He knew that it was somewhat unreasonable of him to have the same expectations of others as he held for himself, but this, he maintained, was common courtesy.

"Hey there, Rog," Diane exclaimed as she flew into Roger's office a moment later, "are you ready to go?" Roger made an exaggerated point of looking at his watch and looked up to meet her gaze: "I've been ready for a few minutes. You were to be here at 10:15!" Roger answered curtly. He liked Diane. She was one of only a handful of people who could call him "Rog."

"Well, I'm not *that* late. I had to finish up with Wendy in Accounting. Sorry," she stated briskly. "Now, let's get a move on, shall we?" she added.

Diane had a nice new car and she was a good driver. Under normal circumstances, Roger enjoyed being the passenger, especially because he loved 'new car smell,' and this one had it in spades. Today was different though. He *knew* they were going to be late and he couldn't do a darn thing about it. Roger hated not having control over situations like these. If they had left, say at ten o'clock, he wouldn't be in the state he was in now and he could have enjoyed the trip.

What made things a bit worse this morning was that Roger got the sense that Diane also knew that they might not make the meeting in time. Her foot was slightly heavier on the gas pedal than usual and she did not engage in the banter that often transpired between them. Sensing this just compounded Roger's agitation and anxiety. At least traffic was on their side: no real hassles or construction delays. In fact, they only had two red lights.

"Shoot," Diane said, perturbed, "there are no spaces left in the parking lot."

Roger could do nothing but stare ahead. It was 10:53. If he didn't get a grip, he was going to lose it. They weren't late... yet. This fact seemed to calm him down a bit. Lucky I didn't have my second cup of coffee, he snickered to himself. He took a couple of deep breaths and noticed a car pulling out of a spot just ahead of them. "Diane, a spot's just opened up. Pull in there and let's go!" he asserted.

Diane expertly manoeuvred the car into the vacant spot, albeit a bit too quickly for Roger's taste. They hopped out and Roger noticed that there was a full hour left on the meter. Hmmm, he uttered to himself, a good omen, perhaps? Diane plunked some quarters into Roger's open palm and asked him to feed the meter even more.

As luck would have it, one of the six elevators in the office tower was voiding itself of its passengers. Diane and Roger, along with three others, skipped in. Roger pushed 42, and the others each pushed another number indicating their floor of choice. Roger shot a quick glance to Diane, and she smirked, knowing exactly what Roger was thinking. The elevator finally stopped on the 42nd floor, where the offices of Reed, Reed, Lubinski and Dixon were located.

Roger looked at his watch: it was exactly 10:59 am.

Emma – *Job Interview Anxiety*

Ryan Westover escorted Emma Chang back to the Human Resources Reception area. "Thank you for coming in and meeting with us, Emma," he said warmly as he extended his hand to complete the transaction. Ryan was the human resources manager and representative who sat on the selection panel with whom Emma had just met.

Emma shook his hand, smiled and said, "Thank you, Mr. Westover."

Ryan turned and retraced his steps back to the interview room. Emma proceeded to make her way to the flight of stairs that would take her down to the lobby of the three-story building.

She'd always liked the building and its location. It was relatively new, modern, very professional in its appearance and just steps to great shopping and restaurants. Tasteful art hung on the walls; the colour scheme was current, muted earth tones with glass and brushed nickel accents, and she noticed a variety of plants of all shapes and sizes, including large palms and ferns, strategically placed around the building, giving it a warm, welcoming feel. She could definitely picture herself working there. She hoped she had a chance. She began thinking about the interview: the panel members, the questions, her answers and examples. In retrospect, it wasn't that bad at all.

Emma was parked in the company's parking lot. She located her car without fail, pressed her remote to unlock her door, and got in behind the wheel. Before turning the key to start the engine, she hesitated for a moment, took a deep breath, and began to reflect on the past forty-eight hours. Looking back, it felt like she had been caught in quite the whirlwind.

The current opportunity had actually presented itself rather quickly. She only became aware of it two weeks ago when she was randomly checking out one or two of the online career sites and she noticed what appeared to be her dream job listed on one. She had to really hustle to get her cover letter and resume together and into the human resources department on time. In fact, the deadline for submissions was the very next day, and had it not been for the fact that Emma always kept a current resume on file, she would have found herself stressed even before she knew she had an interview. If truth be told, Emma updated her resume the very day she started a new job. She liked to be prepared.

Emma was no interview virgin. In her short career, she had experienced her share of job interviews. But, no matter how prepared she was – and she did her research – she always felt extremely anxious leading up to the actual meeting. This anxiety usually began the evening before the interview and lasted until the last question was answered.

Anxiety would set in as a result of the internal voice in her head that would cause her to begin to second-guess herself. Was I the right person for the job? Do I have the right examples? Did I do enough research? What questions will they ask? Will I be able to answer them correctly? What if I freeze up? These thoughts would spring into her mind as soon as she laid her head on her pillow in hopes of getting a good night's sleep.

Emma remembered waking up feeling quite confident. She was competent and motivated. If there were no surprises on their end, she really felt that this could be *the* job. She had eaten a quick and healthy breakfast and then made her way to her closet to lay out her interview ensemble. She planned that as well. As part of her research, Emma had learned that the company had a 'business casual' dress code so she opted for her tailored two-piece powder blue suit, simple black pumps and the small diamond stud earrings that her parents had given her for her last birthday as her only accessory.

She also seemed to remember that the anxiety really took hold while she was getting dressed. It was mild at first, but as she prepared to leave her apartment, her stomach began to churn and her hands began to tremble mildly. She picked up her attaché and purse, locked the door behind her and walked down the one flight of stairs to the ground level of her apartment complex. Her car was stationed just in front of the building. She hopped in, started the ignition and set out.

Ten minutes later Emma found herself turning into the company parking lot. She found a space easily enough, put her car in *Park*, checked her appearance in the rear-view mirror, grabbed her belongings and got out and locked the car. She recalled that it was at this exact moment that she had noticed that her hands were cold and clammy. Great, she chastised herself, now they're going to know that I'm a blundering idiot! She wondered briefly if she could get away with not shaking anyone's hands. Not so much, she decided. She smiled to herself while she thought how comical and awkward that might appear, which took her mind off of the impending interview for a moment. This momentary deflection seemed to ease her anxiety. She pulled herself together, remembered that she was fully prepared and entered the main lobby of the building.

Emma smiled as she remembered when, on the second floor, she had passed the women's washroom on her way to the HR reception area, and had decided to slip in. She rinsed her hands under warm water and dried them using the wall-mounted dryer. This seemed to work: her hands were no longer cold and clammy. She exited the washroom and strode with confidence to the HR department, where she left her name with the receptionist. Within ten minutes, she had been introduced to the four panel members and the interview had begun. That was only seventy-five minutes ago.

That was Wednesday. On Monday of the following week, Emma was notified that she was successful in moving onto the final stage of the selection process: the second interview.

Frank – *Managing 'Millenials' Anxiety*

At 52, Frank didn't consider himself *old* by any stretch of the imagination. He liked his job, and more importantly, knew that he added value to the organization. While retirement was in the not-so-distant future for many of his colleagues, he did not dwell on it like many of them did; counting the months, weeks, and days until they could finally say goodbye and collect their pensions. In fact, Frank really didn't want to retire.

Things at work were changing, though. As employees around the same age were leaving, young, fresh faces were beginning to pop up in all areas of the organization. Frank was one of a significant number of employees within this large municipal organization who was struggling with how to supervise and lead this new breed of worker: the so-called 'millenial.' Frank and his wife of twenty-four years had two kids; a girl, 21, and a boy, 19, so it was not as if he didn't have experience with young adults, he had plenty. He just didn't have experience supervising them at work.

It almost came to a head the other day when, in the midst of a meeting, he noticed one of his apprentices, Tyler, 25, with thumbs tapping ferociously on his iPhone. This wasn't the first time this had happened with Tyler. Up to this point, Frank had just held his breath, overlooking Tyler's apparent disrespectful attitude. However, today, he could barely control himself. Frank started shifting in his chair and began tapping his pen on the table top. Tyler briefly looked up in Franks' direction and must have clued into his annoyance as he quickly hit 'send' and shoved the device deep into his front pants pocket.

The operational planning meeting ended about half an hour later, and Frank left without acknowledging Tyler. He headed straight for his office, dropped his files on his desk and went back out to meet Jim and Chuck for lunch offsite. He was to meet them at 12:30 at a pub nearby.

As he stepped outside, he felt a cool gust of wind swirl around him. It would be fall soon, he thought to himself. He took a few steps and his thoughts soon turned to Tyler, and a couple of the other 'twentysomethings.' He tensed up immediately and he could sense that his blood pressure was rising. He could feel the tension in his upper back, shoulders and neck: it was palpable. It was no wonder he needed a massage practically every week these days. He knew he also lost sleep and important time at work brooding as a result of this stressor.

What is it with these people, anyway? Frank asked himself rhetorically. He just couldn't believe the audacity: Tyler typing on his phone, or 'texting' as they call it, in the middle of a meeting. And that was only one example. He knew of other managers who were experiencing similar problems. Peggy, a manager in Finance, recently told him that one of her clerks basically stormed into her office last Tuesday and practically demanded that she be allowed to take the next two days off because, "the weather was going to be perfect for surfing." Man, he thought to himself, we'd never have been able to get away with anything close to that type of behaviour and expect to keep our jobs when we were that age.

As he neared the pub entrance, Frank relaxed a bit. A good plate of fish and chips and a laugh with the guys would take his mind off of things. Jim waved Frank down as he came through the heavy oak door. As Frank reached the table, he said, "How's it going?" to both Jim and Chuck.

Jim was looking at the lunch specials posted on the blackboard on the wall. Chuck knew what he wanted to eat, so he put the menu on the table, looked Frank square in the eyes, and said, "What's up with these young new hires anyways? Do they think their God's gift or something?"

Chuck must have been reading his mind. "Don't get me started," said Frank, "I'm at my wit's end. I was just at a meeting with one of my apprentices who proceeded to spend at least ten minutes on his blooming iPhone."

Frank started to feel the tension build again and he wanted to change the topic. He shifted in his seat, but just as he was about to say something, Jim piped in. "Guys, let's face it. We are dealing with a different breed of employee," he asserted. Jim had been in management for several years and had the occasion to supervise several 25-30 year olds in the past couple of years. By no means an expert, Jim, however, understood that each generation of employee came with unique character traits, needs, and expectations of what work meant to them.

Frank and Chuck looked in Jim's direction and nodded in agreement. "You sure got that right," admitted Chuck.

Jim continued, "But think for a minute. These guys are probably just as uncomfortable with our generation as we are with theirs."

"Yes," Frank agreed, "but we are their managers; they work for us. They are supposed to do the work that is required of them, and do it with respect." Chuck was nodding vigorously while trying to catch the attention of one of the servers.

"Right, I can see your point." Jim added. "That was how *we* learned to do things. But these folks do things differently. They've grown up differently."

Chuck was about to say something when Frank interrupted, "OK, I'm getting it, Jim. It's like what we learned in that diversity program we took last year. We all bring different things to the table and it is up to us as supervisors to understand what each of our employees brings, whether we are talking generational, educational, or cultural diversity, or whatever."

Jim persisted, saying, "They like to know why they are doing something, and we often fall short in that respect. We should also be open to learning from them, especially when it comes to technology. The first step is having a conversation with them: get to know and understand where they are coming from. Its challenging but it'll help, *and* get easier. I guarantee it." Jim looked at them both and added, "I know that you two are up for it!"

Frank and Chuck hesitated for a moment, considering Jim's words. They finally looked at each other and nodded agreement. Frank shrugged his shoulders and said, "what's one more challenge, eh Chuck?"

Rachel – *Forgetting To Do Things Anxiety*

Nancy noticed a flash of colour whiz by her office as she began to pack up for the night. She recognized Rachel's mass of red hair out of the corner of her eye, as if it was a large fire ball racing to catch up with the woman herself.

"Hey, where's the fire?" Nancy blurted as she popped out of her office door to see if she could catch Rachel.

"Gotta' run, Nance! I'm late, I'll see you tomorrow!" Rachel retorted, raising her free hand in a dismissive wave without even turning her head. Nancy looked at her watch; it was only a few minutes after five.

Moments earlier Rachel had been sitting at her computer, deep in concentration, editing the proposal she was trying to get ready for the following day. All of the sudden, panic struck and she looked at the clock located in the bottom right hand corner of her computer screen. "Crap," she said out loud, "double crap!" Late again. How could I forget? she berated herself. She began to feel mad at and disappointed in herself. She could feel her heart rate start to increase.

She quickly put her desktop computer in sleep mode and straightened up a few loose items on her desk. She stood up, grabbed her mobile phone, laptop, gym bag, purse and keys. Running out of her office, she pulled the handle a bit too hard and heard the door slam as she was sprinting down the corridor. She vaguely remembers hearing Nancy's voice as she darted past her office. I hope I wasn't too rude, she thought to herself.

She glanced at the clock that was hanging on the wall behind the reception desk as she checked in for her appointment. It read 5:28. The appointment was at 5:30 and she didn't like to be late. After all, it was her massage appointment, and she'd been looking forward to it all day. She had a couple of minutes to unwind before she was escorted by the receptionist to her massage room, promptly at 5:30.

Her 60-minute massage began on time. The massage therapist was gentle but firm. Rachel began to allow her body and mind to relax. She needed this; she'd been feeling a lot of work-related stress lately. For some reason, she was forgetting to get things done at work, and this caused her some tension that she needed released.

She had succumbed to the gentle kneading and squeezing. The lavender aromatherapy oil was soothing as it drifted around the room and the soft tones of the spa-like music lulled Rachel into a state of sheer contentment.

"Oh my Gosh!" she exploded out of the blue, pulling both herself and the therapist out of the trance-like atmosphere the room now manifested.

While Rachel lifted her head from the massage table 'donut', Sven, the therapist, alarmed, raised his hands from Rachel's back and asked, "Rachel, is everything OK?"

"I'm such a blinking idiot," she responded as the words came out of her mouth before she could filter them. She did not like the words she used to describe herself just then.

"What's up?" Sven enquired.

"For starters, when I was racing out of the office this afternoon I forgot to save the document I've been working on all day," she started to explain, "and it's a product of about four solid days of work. I also forgot to make travel arrangements for a meeting I'm attending next week."

"Well," said Sven, "I'm no techie, but can't you retrieve the file somehow? Are you sure you lost your day's work?"

In the moment, Rachel couldn't recollect whether she'd saved the document: whether she had shut down her system completely, or whether she had just hit 'sleep.' If she hadn't saved the document, she'd be out of a day's work, and it was due tomorrow. She couldn't think clearly. And how was it that she *just* remembered now about the business meeting next week? Stupid, stupid, stupid, she lamented, now completely beside herself, tense and full of dread that she may have missed the mark.

Sven proceeded carefully. He offered, "Rachel, can you really do anything at this moment about these things? Is worrying about them tonight going to help matters?"

Rachel knew where Sven was heading, and appreciated his calmness. She realized that she would probably brood about this the entire evening, but she decided then and there that she was going to try to put these problems out of her mind, so that she could at least enjoy the rest of her massage. She turned her head toward Sven and said, "Let's continue. I'm sorry for the outburst!" and quickly plunked her head back into the 'donut.'

Sven quickly began to help Rachel to regain her sense of calm using every technique and trick he had up his sleeve as a professional massage therapist. He leaned over Rachel and whispered in her ear, "Don't worry, it happens all the time."

Rachel, in mild disbelief, responded, "Right!"

Sven continued, "You wouldn't believe where people go in their minds while they are having a massage. Some people actually have me stop so they can jot an idea or a note down. Funny, but it happens."

Rachel gave herself permission to enjoy the rest of the massage. As she was leaving, she thanked Sven, settled the payment and tip with the receptionist, made her next appointment, and left.

On her way home, she made a detour back to the office. She wanted to be sure that she had saved her work and she knew she'd have a fitful sleep if she didn't at least check. If it was gone, she'd have to pull an all-nighter.

Her heart was racing as she approached her office door. All the way to the office, she prayed to the gods. Please, please, please! played the litany in her head. She unlocked her door and pressed the spacebar on her keyboard. To her delight (and immense relief), the machine was in 'sleep' mode, and her proposal quickly sprang to life on her screen. "Thank you!" she exclaimed as if the monitor were a human being. She saved the document – both on her hard drive and on her memory stick.

Taking out a fresh piece of paper, Rachel sat down and made a list of things she needed to do.

Paul & Lara — *Clean vs. Cluttered Anxiety*

T hey couldn't be more opposite," Jerry remarked to his executive assistant, Debra, as he was leaning against the door frame to his office. He was, of course, talking about Paul and Lara, two of his senior managers. Debra looked up from her computer screen at Jerry, inquisitively. "You just have to look at their offices. The clues are right there!" Jerry persisted. "Paul's is spotless, which I must say sometimes makes me wonder, and Lara's is so cluttered and disorganized I'd be surprised if she could find anything in the chaos." Debra smiled back at Jerry. She liked both Paul and Lara, but it was funny how opposite they were in that regard.

Paul detested a disorganized working environment. He preferred an office that was in order, clean and functional. For him to be effective in his job, Paul needed to have a place for everything and everything had to be in its place. He felt comfortable in a clean, uncluttered environment. He could think straight and not be distracted by notes strewn here and there; files stacked haphazardly all around the office; or toys, pictures and office 'swag' clogging up his desk, credenza and shelving surfaces. A clean office, for him, represented peace, order, and function: the means to peak performance. A cluttered office represented pandemonium, confusion and madness: a direct route to misery.

Debra fondly remembered Paul's first day of work. He was not in his office for a minute before he ran out looking white as a ghost in search of a glass of water. Debra pointed to the water cooler and waited at his door until he returned a few moments later. She recalled that his forehead was covered in sweat and his hands were trembling so much that he spilled most of the water that was left in the glass. She lightly placed her hand on his forearm to steady it. She remembered telling him to breathe and relax.

"Relax?" he responded incredulously, "have you seen the mess in there?" Debra smirked knowing that the previous occupant, Henry Drummond, was not the tidiest of people.

"Oh, no, the door's been closed since Henry left a week or so ago, and I wasn't sure if I should touch anything knowing that you'd be taking his place," she admitted.

"I suppose it was too much for him to tidy up a bit?" enquired Paul with sarcasm.

"Let's see," Debra uttered as she neared Paul's office. "Oh Paul, this *is* tidy!" she added, noticing Paul's expression of disbelief and horror as his hands began twitching again uncontrollably.

In the five minutes that Paul was acclimatizing himself to his new surroundings, he began breathing quickly and feeling flushed. He circled around the space feeling a bit dizzy and unsure of where to start. Things of all shapes and sizes – from files to books to staplers to cups proudly displaying the company logo – were scattered without sense or reasoning all over the modestly sized office. All of the sudden, panic, dread and the feeling that he was drowning overtook him. It was at that moment that he hurried toward the door in search of water.

Fifteen minutes later, he and Debra were sifting through the office's contents, slowing putting things in order. Debra was happy to oblige because she knew it was going to make her job easier in the long run, and she didn't think it was fair that Paul should have to put up with Henry's mess. She was a calming influence and knew the business, so could offer her perspectives when needed. They worked together for the better part of the morning reclassifying the filing system, sorting and purging years of old and valueless documents and folders, cleaning and rearranging surfaces to Paul's inclination, all with the sole purpose of re-establishing a sense of order and calm.

The next day, Lara, who had been a part of Jerry's management team for four years, stopped by Paul's office to introduce herself. Paul's door was open, yet she knocked lightly on the doorframe so she wouldn't startle him.

"Hello, I'm guessing you're Paul Preston," she said: more a statement than a question.

Paul turned and looked up from his computer screen meeting Lara's gaze. He hesitated for a split second, stood up and crossed the room with his hand extended. "At your service," he quipped light-heartedly.

"Lara Toombs," she said as she offered her hand. "My office is next to yours. I wasn't in yesterday but I wanted to introduce myself before Jerry does the formal intros later on this morning."

"Glad to meet you," Paul added.

From her vantage point, Lara could take in Paul's entire office. Her eyes did a sweep of the surroundings. She blinked, and began to feel restless. "Wow," she commented, "starting from a blank slate?"

"Well," replied Paul energetically, "you should've seen this place yesterday. What a mess. No disrespect to Henry, but I couldn't work in that kind of chaos." He continued, "Debra and I spent most of the day turning this place around. I can actually breathe now."

Lara thought she was going to lose it. She had always admired Henry's ability to juggle: files, projects, assignments – you name it. She couldn't help herself when she said judgmentally, "I don't see how anyone can work this way, Paul. There's not a file folder in sight. No papers. No note pads," she observed. "How on earth do you get any work done?" she asked rhetorically. "How could anyone find anything in such a sterile space?"

For Lara, a desk that was void of files, papers, stick-it notes, cups and water bottles, a family photo or two, gave her the impression of someone who was lazy, workshy, not creative nor productive – someone who, as far as she was concerned, was quite useless. Clutter and disarray symbolized hard work, imagination and resourcefulness. She knew that she was on the verge of hyperventilating, so she abruptly excused herself, saying, "Nice meeting you. See you at the meeting."

Paul was momentarily stunned. He returned to his chair, sat down and swivelled around, giving his office a nod of approval.

Michelle – *Loss of Employment Anxiety*

Raj met Michelle in the cafeteria of the organization's multi-level compound shortly after 1 pm. They met to have lunch and to discuss the rumours that were spreading like wildfire. Michelle didn't like the rumour mill, especially when it contained inklings of mergers, downsizing, restructuring or re-engineering. And in this economy, anything was possible.

"Over here," Raj shouted to Michelle, flagging her down as the cashier handed her back the debit card she used to pay for her lunch. Michelle nodded, picked up her utensils and other sundries, and made her way over to one of the coveted window tables that Raj had grabbed from a trio of 'twentysomethings' who had just packed up to leave. "Don't forget your garbage," he said to them, smiling.

They settled into seats facing each other and started to eat. After a few minutes, Michelle couldn't wait any longer and pleaded, "Raj, come on, tell me what's going on."

Raj swallowed a bite of his meal, glanced up and saw that Michelle was glaring at him from across the table. He teased, "Whatever do you mean, Michelle?"

"Fine, have it your way," she said with determination as she slammed her fork onto the table for dramatic effect. "We'll just sit, eat our lunch, and then go on our merry way."

"Rather melodramatic, eh Michelle?" he said, smirking at her. She ignored him as she grabbed her can of diet soda and took a drink, avoiding eye contact.

"OK, ok… I'll tell you what I know, but there really isn't much to tell," admitted Raj. "We are looking at reorganizing a couple of divisions to better respond to market demands. No surprise, really. The organization does that to keep current; we've done it before."

"Not since I've been here, we haven't," Michelle interjected in a nervous tone. She noticed that she was beginning to experience dry mouth, and she was getting fidgety, playing with her food rather than eating it.

Raj noticed this subtle change in her demeanour and determined that this was a sensitive topic for Michelle. He proceeded cautiously. He asked, "Mich, why are you letting this bother you? Nothing is set in stone. They are months from making any final decisions. Regardless, your job is secure. In fact, no one will be laid off."

"Yeah, I've heard that before," responded Michelle, suspiciously.

Michelle had never lost any of her positions of employment, even amidst company downsizing, redundancies and lay-offs. She'd always been able to maintain her employment status. Nevertheless, she lived in a constant state of worry that she was going to lose her job and, therefore, not be able to support herself.

"Where is this all coming from, Michelle?" Raj asked, genuinely interested in trying to understand Michelle's apprehension. "Why so anxious?"

Michelle began, "Well, I think it stems from two separate, but related, reasons. Growing up," she continued, "we had very limited money in our family. We weren't poor or anything, but my parents had to watch every cent. When I graduated from high school, I immediately went to college and worked at a part-time job. I had to make it on my own. My parents couldn't afford much in the way of financial support. Even in my early twenties, I didn't have the opportunity of going back to live with my parents. It just wasn't possible, and I didn't want to be an extra burden on them, anyway." She stopped, allowing herself to gather her thoughts, and took another bite of her lunch.

"OK, and you've made it. Look at where you are now!" acknowledged Raj, knowing that she was pulling in a great salary, had an awesome condo nestled on the outskirts of the city, and drove a newer model Audi A4. "It seems to me that you have nothing to concern yourself about," he added.

"Right, you'd think that, but I start feeling anxious and worried – I can even feel my heart race as we speak – when I hear of restructuring or downsizing, or of anything that may jeopardize my security," Michelle persevered. "And, when I split up from my partner, Rob, two years ago, it took me a long time to realize that I could support myself without a second income. And that was fine for a while until I began to think about what would happen if I lost *my* job."

Raj listened attentively. He took this opportunity to jump in and say, "Michelle, nothing is guaranteed in this life except death and taxes." She tilted her head and stared at him for a moment with a sarcastic smirk on her face before continuing.

"I know I take myself too seriously at times – like right now – and during these times I tend to over analyze my situation when I know I should just trust myself and, as they say, the *process*," she said with emphasis. "I think that my anxiety stems from my perception of my ability to maintain a sense of order. You know, what I can control within my own environment. I've never been without employment but I know this fear hinders me from launching my own consultancy," she admitted introspectively. "I couldn't even imagine not knowing exactly where my next paycheque was coming from."

"You got that right," Raj agreed, "however, thousands of people do it, and very successfully!" He waited another moment. "So, how do you cope with this anxiety, Mich?" he finally asked with mild concern.

"Oh, talking it through really helps, so thanks, Raj," she answered. "When it rears its ugly face, I try to exercise and rationalize my thoughts through positive self-talk to put me back into the right frame of mind. I also try to get as much information as I can about the situation," she continued. "And, having a nice savings account helps!" she said, smiling as Raj turned in her direction, matching her smile with one of his own.

Ted – 'Have I Done A Good Job?' Anxiety

B ruce was slowly making his way around the boardroom table providing feedback to members of his team. There were twelve people in all; most of whom were hard working, high producing members of his graphics design and publishing team. The team had, in the past, gone through significant change in terms of its member make up, but for the past eight months or so, things seemed to have settled down. Everyone seemed challenged, motivated, and happy to be a part of this innovative, high performing team.

Bruce was proud of his team's accomplishments, and the admiration was mutual. Bruce was considered a skilled and thoughtful leader, always willing to chip in and listen to ideas while at the same time ensuring the tasks were completed and that the talent of his team members was being utilized to the fullest.

Ted was sitting… waiting. At first, he began to fidget. He lifted his cup, pulled out the small square napkin that was underneath it, and started folding it as if he were an origami master. When that didn't calm him down, he began to doodle. And doodling was not a good sign. When Ted began to doodle, he knew that it was an indication that he was pulling away, retreating into his thoughts, distancing himself from the others. He was aware of what was transpiring around him; he could hear Bruce's kind comments and accolades in the background, but he was not a part of the action. At least he didn't pull out his mobile device to take his mind off things; that would have meant certain death by embarrassment.

He began to get tense; he could feel his body stiffen. Bruce was almost finished giving his compliments, and Ted had not yet been mentioned. In fact, Bruce had actually skipped Ted as he worked his way through most – albeit not all – of his colleagues.

Ted enjoyed getting feedback. More importantly, Ted craved receiving positive feedback. Anything less than rave reviews would cause Ted to second-guess himself: to question whether he was up for the challenge at hand, or the work for which he was currently responsible. When Ted didn't receive feedback indicating that he has done a great job – not just good, but 'great' – or when he believed he heard insinuations that he had done a less than stellar job, or that his clients or colleagues were less than *very* pleased, he would quiver in his uncertainty and begin to lose confidence in himself, which often left him feeling isolated and disempowered. It was so bad that, a few years ago, after not receiving feedback of any kind from his manager for several months, Ted actually thought of quitting his job.

Mid-doodle, Ted thought he heard his name. He drifted back into the conversation mid-sentence.

"…and without Ted's innovative and inspiring initial concept design, we may still be at the drawing board," Bruce commented proudly while looking at Ted.

Ted was taken aback. He was dumbfounded but managed to sit up and become a part of the conversation again. It only took him a split second to catapult himself out of his internal downward spiral and into this reverie of praise in this moment. He flushed mildly: this time, not from the trepidation and internal angst of not being recognized, but from the praise and recognition itself, and from the mild embarrassment he felt knowing that all eyes were on him.

Bruce continued, "Ted, I want to take this opportunity to thank you and your team for acting as a catalyst for this project. For a split second, I bet you thought I had overlooked, you, right?" Bruce pointed at Ted, smiling, and Ted responded with a short, nondescript shake of his head, feeling somewhat humiliated.

Ted continued to blush as he basked in the warmth he was feeling from Bruce and his colleagues. He knew the recognition was sincere, which, of course, made it all the better.

Back in his office, Ted reflected for a few moments about what transpired in the boardroom. He couldn't help but feel both stupid and silly, thinking, how could I have let my thoughts run away from me so completely? Geesh – the assumptions I made! And I made them so quickly only to be proven that they were wrong.

Ted remembered something his professional coach once clarified for him: that perceptions are not only our 'reality' but they are also our projections. I certainly fell into that trap, didn't I? he thought to himself. I went so easily to that place of worry and anxiety that I was not going to be recognized, that I virtually shut down. In this reflective state, he realized, Not only is that bad news for me and my sanity, but it's also not so good on so many other levels: for my colleagues, for Bruce, for the team.

Remembering back on the times he had been caught in this anxiety, Ted soon realized that it had all stemmed from his perception of things: his projection of the reality that surrounded him. Not that his view of reality was wrong, necessarily – at least from his perspective – but he needed to check it out with others to be sure he had the whole story. My own thoughts, doubt, and uncertainty can get me into a lot of trouble, he thought to himself, if I allow them to. To make matters worse, or better – depending on the side from which you were looking at the situation – Ted realized that he was successful, that he had never really received anything less than reaffirming, positive feedback.

From now on, Ted declared to himself, I'm going to remind myself of these things before I jump to conclusions. Further yet, if I don't get feedback when I think it's deserved, I'm going to take a risk and ask for it. Realizing this empowered Ted. All he had to do was ask.

Ainsley – *T e c h n o l o g y   A n x i e t y*

She quickly walked into the classroom. She was already late. Ainsley always liked to arrive at least a full hour before her class was scheduled to begin. She liked this time to ease into the day and set up: arrange tables, chairs, flipchart easels; power up her laptop and LCD projector, and any other technical equipment she may need for the day. But today, the traffic was horrendous and what would have taken her thirty minutes under normal circumstances took her almost forty-five. "Darn construction," she said under her breath as she deposited her armloads of bags and cases onto the desk that was next to her.

Ainsley was a contractor and provided instruction and facilitation services for a couple of the local colleges in her area. Her specialty was leadership, team and communication effectiveness, and she enjoyed both the content and the ability to engage with the diverse range of students who enrolled in her courses.

While she wanted to inform the program coordinator that she would be late to arrive – and beg for her assistance – she was unable to do so en route. It wasn't that she was worried about breaking the 'no speaking on the cell phone while driving' law. The fact was that she had at least three opportunities to pull over and make a quick call legally. No, it was that she was unable to get any cell reception. This upset caused Ainsley to feel a mild increase in her heart rate: the same sort of jump in her adrenaline that she felt after her third cup of caffeine. While not altogether unpleasant, this feeling was nonetheless usually a precursor to unwelcome jitters.

Realizing that she had barely fifteen minutes within which to completely set up, she hastily began to unpack her supplies. She had a lot of supplies. Too many, she thought to herself. Why do I need to bring so much stuff? It took her a few moments, but she managed to arrange her supplies, the tables, and other learning materials the way she had originally intended.

Now, it was onto the technical pieces. Ainsley loved technology – when it worked. Lucky for her, it worked most of the time. However, still to this day, each and every time she approached her laptop or LCD machine – or anything electronic that she relied upon – her heart skipped a beat. She often let technology get the best of her. She didn't control technology; in her mind, technology controlled her, and she didn't like that one bit. She couldn't explain it. She knew what to do and was somewhat comfortable with the technology she used. Perhaps it was that she relied too heavily on it. According to Ainsley, technology provided such a variety of media within which to engage the participant that she felt it would be a disservice to instruct without it.

She focused her attention on her media. She quickly plugged in her laptop and LCD projector. Ainsley inhaled as if gasping and experienced a brief moment of panic. She couldn't remember which she had to turn on first. There was an order – a sequence – that if performed correctly would enable successful blast-off, but she couldn't remember what it was: the laptop first or the LCD? Concentrate, Ainsley, she begged herself, concentrate!

At that moment, four participants entered the classroom, a coffee from the nearest trendy coffee shop in each of their hands.

"Good morning," greeted Ainsley, sincerely, as she looked up and smiled at each participant in turn. "Welcome, my name is Ainsley Ravenhill!" Each participant returned her greeting with their respective names and took a seat.

Ainsley quickly returned to the task at hand, becoming increasingly agitated. All machines were powered up, but she must have made an error in judgment and initially turned the wrong one on first. Blast it! she scolded herself. She quickly unplugged the two machines to try again. After waiting the allotted shutdown time, she went through the start up process again. This time, she used the correct sequence. However, while the LCD projected correctly onto the large screen, Ainsley's computer screen showed a black void. Ainsley sighed and looked at the clock hanging on the wall directly over the classroom door. It read 8:58 am. Class began at 9:00 am.

Lucky for me, she told herself, three-quarters of the class haven't arrived yet.

For the next few minutes, participants trickled into the room, taking their seats and exchanging pleasantries. Ainsley was focused on her task trying to get her computer screen's display to show when one of the students asked if she needed assistance.

"Well, um, thanks, if you could?" replied Ainsley in desperation. She liked to start on time, or at most a few minutes past the official start time on the first day of class, leaving participants the opportunity to navigate parking and get accustomed to the college's maze of corridors.

"You see, these laptops are all different in how they toggle between media," explained Sheila, one of Ainsley's new participants. Sheila pushed a key once, and then the same key again, which illuminated the laptop screen, to Ainsley's delight.

"Thanks *so* much," replied Ainsley. "When I'm under pressure, I seem to lose all logic."

Sheila retraced her steps and took her seat. Moments later, all eighteen participants were comfortably seated and eager to begin. Ainsley straightened herself out and regained her composure. Everything works out in the end, she thought to herself, remembering that her father used the exact same phrase as words of encouragement in her teenage years.

It would happen again: technology anxiety, that is. Would she be prepared for it? Probably not. Was she going to worry about it now? Absolutely not!

Qila – *A b a n d o n m e n t   A n x i e t y*

Nadia and Alex were slowly gathering up supplies for their quick trip into town. Water, check. Protein bars, check. Recyclable grocery bags, check. Cell phone, check. Grocery and video list, check. Check, check, check.

Qila knew something was up. She always knew when her Mom and Dad were leaving to go somewhere. They would always run around like chickens. They would pile stuff on the hallway bench so they wouldn't forget. However, most times they would forget her, or abandon her. Maybe not this time, she seemed to think to herself.

Qila began pacing: to the front door, back down the hallway through to the kitchen, back to the front door, repeat. Several times she would do this, which made her even more anxious and uptight. Maybe if they see that I want to go with them… maybe if they see me walk to the front door, they will take me this time… Qila hoped.

Arms full of their required supplies, Nadia and Alex locked the door and walked along the winding pathway to the red station wagon parked on the gravel parking pad. Both of them looked back simultaneously and waved toward the front door, seeing Qila's beautiful face as she pressed her nose against the glass.

It was a French door, consisting of a full pane of clear glass, so Qila could see the two of them making their grand gesture of waving good-bye to her, probably thinking that the wave would be a suitable facsimile to her actually accompanying them on their errands.

Qila liked going on errands. She always saw so much and usually met such interesting people who were enamoured with her, which she secretly loved. She thought that riding in the car was an absolute thrill, especially with the sunroof open. In the car, she was never far away from the two most favourite people in her life, the two who she most adored in the entire world. Being away from them left such a void in her heart. At the moment that the car swung around the bend, Qila wondered if they would ever come back.

Nadia and Alex didn't always leave Qila behind, and felt badly that they had to today. They made sure they had given her a treat, and made doubly sure that they waved good-bye to her before they hopped into the car, noticing that she was looking at them with such big, sad, brown eyes through the door's full length pane of glass. Qila's expression of pure, sincere sadness always pulled at Nadia's heart strings.

Alex saw Nadia's expression and said, "Wow, she really knows how to lay it on thick, doesn't she?" tilting his head in the direction of the front door.

Nadia smiled as she turned around to face the front of the car. As they navigated the turn in the road, they both crooked their necks so that they could see the door. Having made this a part of their departing ritual, they both knew full well what to expect. Nothing. Qila was nowhere to be seen.

"Well, so much for that!" said Nadia as they drove down the lane. "I guess she's over it."

Qila's good-bye glance at the front door was sincere, albeit short. While she didn't know for sure that they would be returning, she did know that she needed to catch up on some well-deserved shut-eye. She pranced into the living room and bounced on the couch. She dug into the soft seat to mould the perfect spot to take a bit of a siesta. She liked the fact that Nadia left a couple of cushions on the couch. She buried her nose under one, sighed heavily and seemed to let her abandonment anxiety float away as she drifted into a perfect dog-nap.

And, by the way, Nadia and Alex did return!

Anxiety – A Brief MindBody Perspective

Anxiety is an uneasiness of mind often related to an anticipated or impending situation or outcome. It is an emotion of apprehension, fear or discomfort and may even be accompanied by physiological signs like sweating or an increased heart rate.

For the most part, anxiety is caused by a fear of a future event, sometimes identifiable and sometimes not. It can range from mild to severe when it can manifest as a full-blown panic attack or even a disabling isolation and a psychological breakdown if the anxiety is not attended to.

Adrenaline (also known as epinephrine) is the hormone we produce which is involved in our physiological response to stress and elevated levels can result in the physical manifestations of anxiety:

- Increased heart rate (tachycardia)
- High blood pressure
- Sweating
- Abdominal cramps
- Dry mouth (salivary gland inhibition)
- Dilated pupils.

Anxiety is a very common feeling which we all experience and deal with on some level with varying intensity. It can encompass a moment's discomfort about being late for an appointment or a more lasting uneasiness about the consequences of having made a mistake. It can also be a sustained, all-encompassing feeling of fear and dread about a decision to be taken or a choice we have already made.

Whatever the anxiety, the key to its management is *AWARENESS;* becoming mindful of the nervousness, fears, discomforts and dis-eases we each have inside. This entails understanding how often these are present, what intensity they have and how they affect the quality of our lives.

Awareness on a regular daily basis is so very important because it is the unattended-to small anxieties that can, over time, become the reservoir source of our unexplained panic, negativity, unfathomable darkness and senseless desperation.

Once acknowledged and understood, we can begin to deal with the anxiety we have inside. This may include some of the following:

1. Meditation... training the mind to let go.
2. Conscious breathing (belly breathing, qi gong, yoga breathing)... this helps us bring mind and body together in relaxation and gets us out of the repetitive anxious thought mindset.
3. Slowing down... doing too much too fast fuels anxiety.

4. Exercise and sweating... helps us get out of our anxious minds.

5. Counselling... sometimes we need professional help.

6. Getting our troubles off our chests... when we release and let go of our anxieties, we open the pressure release valve. Keeping it inside is toxic to our systems.

7. Good sleep... rest and rejuvenation allow us to heal mind and body.

8. More laughter and not taking ourselves too seriously. Laugher is, after all, the best medicine and it helps to remember that we are just small temporary pulses in a truly massive universe.

9. Actually feeling what the full extent of the anxiety does in our bodies in a safe environment, with or without a mentor/counsellor. This is helpful because we have the opportunity to realize that the full thrust of the anxiety is not going to do us in.

10. More balance in our lives... with balance, there is harmony and with harmony, there is more peace and less anxiety.

Anxiety is in us all and affects us all in various ways. It can also affect us differently at various times of our lives. Being mindful and using a mixture of the techniques listed above on a daily basis can keep you healthy and in mind-body balance.

© Howard Koseff, M.D.

Dr. Howard Koseff

Dr. Koseff lives and belly breathes in North America with his wife, Lauri, and German Shepherd, Flecha (both are belly breathers, too!). He is a medical doctor and a MindBody blogger (www.drmindbodyisin.com).

CDs created by Dr. Koseff

"Distress or De-Stress?" will help you learn to belly breathe. It will also help you learn to do a body scan and to detoxify. For those of you with insomnia, the last track will help you fall asleep without drugs.

This CD "It's all in the breath!" will help you find your healer within, transform your chronic pain and melt your anger away. The last track will leave you feeling full of acceptance and grace.

To order one of these wonderful CDs or learn more about Dr. Koseff and his passion, be sure to visit his websites: www.bellybreathe.com and www.drmindbodyisin.com.

Garry Brookes | Illustrator/Animator

Garry Brookes is an Illustrator and Animator from Vancouver British Columbia. He graduated from Vancouver Film School where he completed both their 'Traditional' and 'Digital' animation programs.

Garry has worked on several short films and is constantly working on new exciting projects. He also participates in several online Artist communities. In 2011 he was chosen to represent Vancouver Film School as an alumni/animator at 'Siggraph Vancouver' (The world's premier conference on computer graphics and interactive techniques). Garry's inspiration comes from all the great people he surrounds himself with including family, friends and fellow artists.

A New Anxiety Questionnaire!

Follow the link below to access the new online anxiety questionnaire. Complete the confidential questionnaire and share your anxiety story.

If your story is used in a subsequent version of "The Anxiety Chronicles", you will receive a free copy!

> "I thought it was incredibly therapeutic to reflect and intentionally write about my anxiety"
> Connie, Seattle
>
> "I found that answering the questions on the survey lifted my spirits"
> David, Vancouver
>
> "It is great knowing that I can share my story so that others know that they are not alone"
> Barb, Surrey

The Anxiety Questionnaire can be found at:

https://www.surveymonkey.com/s/anxietyquestionnaire

Complete the questionnaire now!